YOUR MARRIAGE TODAY

...AND TOMORROW

MAKING YOUR RELATIONSHIP MATTER NOW
AND FOR GENERATIONS TO COME

CRAWFORD & KAREN LORITTS

FOREWORD BY GARY CHAPMAN

#1 *New York Times* bestselling author of *The 5 Love Languages*®

Praise for *Your Marriage Today . . . and Tomorrow*

We need a strong voice anchored in truth to call us back to what really matters when a man and a woman say, "I do." I do not know a couple more qualified and capable of pointing us in the right direction than Crawford and Karen Loritts. Their faithful lives in ministry and marriage have already been a well-written book, drafted with intentionality and attention to God-honoring detail. Now, decades into the journey, the lessons they've garnered and the generational impact they've created for their own family is at our fingertips within the pages of this book.

This is the compass we've been looking for. Theirs is the voice that we need and it's the one I'm listening to. You should too.

PRISCILLA SHIRER
Author and Bible teacher

Crawford and Karen are at once relatable and convicting, funny, and wise. Through this timely book, they show us how husbands and wives do more than build a family; they leave a gospel legacy. Marriage and parenting done God's way can be the greatest contribution we can make to the Great Commission. We will send our children to places we can never go—most notably, the future. If you want your marriage to be infused with the power that Jesus promises will accompany the Great Commission, don't just read, but spend time with this helpful book.

J. D. GREEAR
Pastor, The Summit Church, Raleigh-Durham, NC

Crawford and Karen's passion for giving hope is contagious and one for us all to model. In *Your Marriage Today . . . and Tomorrow* their heart for mentoring shines through. Crawford and Karen remind us that our marriage relationships leave a legacy. What will it be? Thoughtful and inspiring, you'll find treasures of encouragement to invest in your marriage today as a way to bless the marriages of tomorrow. Rhonda, my wife of forty-five years in 2018, joins me in sharing our best wishes to Crawford and Karen as they encourage and nurture marriages, families, and future generations for years to come.

DAN CATHY
President/CEO, Chick-fil-A

I have known Karen and Crawford for over forty years. I am so glad that they have given us a hope-filled road map to encourage us in developing marriages that will bless generations to come.

JOHN PERKINS
Founder and President Emeritus of the John & Vera Mae Perkins Foundation

As a still fairly newlywed myself (married at age fifty-seven!), I was delighted to learn that Crawford and Karen had written this book, and was eager to read it and learn from their wisdom. I've known this couple for many years and they are two of my favorite people. The very different backgrounds they brought to their marriage could have been a recipe for a less than ideal future. But by God's grace, their marriage has gone the distance and is a beautiful reflection of the gospel story. They have been intentional about passing on to their children and grandchildren a rare, precious legacy of devotion to Christ. This book is warm, personal, insightful, thought-provoking, practical, and above all robustly biblical. I heartily commend it to every believer who cares about experiencing and sharing with others a vision for marriage as God intended it to be.

NANCY DeMOSS WOLGEMUTH
Author, teacher, and host of *Revive Our Hearts*

Any time I have a conversation with Crawford Loritts, I come away with much needed perspective. He's one of those guys who opens his mouth and just lets wisdom flow from it, effortlessly and graciously. *Your Marriage Today . . . and Tomorrow* comes from the heart, gleaned from a marriage of nearly fifty years. The first thing I thought was this should be required reading for all newlyweds. And then I realized that as a man who has been married for thirty-five years, I was learning things that will serve me and my wife well for years and years to come. Well done, Crawford . . . again.

ERNIE JOHNSON JR.
TNT Sportscaster; author of *NY Times* bestseller *Unscripted*

Crawford and Karen Loritts have ministered to countless couples wanting to follow God's design for their marriage. And they practice what they preach! Their stories will give you hope and their ideas will give you tools for creating a marriage built to last!

TONY EVANS
Senior Pastor, Oak Cliff Bible Fellowship and President, The Urban Alternative

Through candid backstory and reflection, as well as deep wells of wisdom and experience, Crawford and Karen give helpful pathways to keep your marriage growing so that it overflows and expresses Jesus to rising generations. This book is a timely and important resource to help your marriage be a "sacred conduit" to continue to grow God's kingdom.

DAVID ROBBINS
President and CEO of FamilyLife

Your Marriage Today . . . and Tomorrow is one of those rare books I'll read after seeing the "movie." My life has been profoundly shaped by my folks, and I couldn't be more thrilled you get the chance to catch the overflow of what me and my siblings received.

BRYAN LORITTS
Lead Pastor, Abundant Life; author of *Saving the Saved*

God's design for marriage goes way beyond the two of you! Here Crawford and Karen Loritts unpack God's Word, honestly share their own stories, and offer life-changing principles to show you how to build a marriage with impact for life and eternity.

JOSH D. McDOWELL
Author and speaker

When I heard Crawford and Karen Loritts were writing a book on marriage, I was thrilled. They have been friends for many years, and I know they have a lot to share. What is particularly encouraging is their approach: how a good marriage can have a purpose and mission that will influence not only children and grandchildren, but also subsequent generations and others besides. This is a powerful book for people who want their marriages to count for eternity.

STEVE DOUGLASS
President, Campus Crusade for Christ International/Cru

I've been to the conferences and I've heard the talks. However, nothing beats having watched the truths in this book lived out in front of me. Blessed beyond measure to have these examples.

HEATHER LORITTS

Crawford and Karen Loritts have been married for more four and a half decades and walked with Jesus even longer. That combination alone warrants a read! I know all of his children and have been a fan and, in my mind, an adopted son of this family. It's easy to read the stories and hear the word of God about family through them. Not only do you get their story, but you get the redemptive story of the gospel woven into this work. Read and use it as a lifetime reference tool for marriage!

ERIC MASON
Lead Pastor and founder, Epiphany Fellowship

A beautiful reminder that "marriage and family are intended to be a reflection and portrait of the oneness and love found in the Trinity." This book challenges us to relentlessly pursue a Christ-honoring marriage that is selfless and forgiving and always seeking a deeper level of intimacy. By faithfully modeling these behaviors, Crawford and Karen give hope to the next generation.

BUBBA AND CINDY CATHY
EVP and President of Dwarf House / Chick-fil-A, Inc.

Crawford and Karen are the real deal. As usual their instruction is spot on. But it is the reality of their lives together and their families before and after them that make their timeless teachings an authentic resource that can be trusted for the challenges that face us all in marriage, family, and life itself.

BARRY AND ANGELYN CANNADA
Chairman, Board of Directors, Campus Crusade International/Cru

Marriage can either be a source of great peace and joy or, unfortunately for some, conflict and sorrow. So learning to manage marriage toward positive outcomes is vitally important. Thankfully, my friends Crawford and Karen Loritts have charted a course to follow based on biblical wisdom and practical experience. Whether your marriage is thriving or struggling, you will find their insights to be of great benefit. Highly recommended!

JOE STOWELL
President, Cornerstone University

All my life I have watched my parents literally live out these truths in this book. Even though they're not perfect, there's a profound sense of wanting to honor the Lord in everything, especially in their marriage. Through ups and downs, in victory and in failure, their commitment to the Lord and to each other has imprinted me and my siblings' lives. I am grateful for the legacy they have stewarded, modeled, and passed to us. Sometimes I wish people could see greatness in "private" because that's what I have witnessed. Thank you mom and dad. I love you dearly!

BRYNDAN LORITTS
Senior Pastor, Harvest Bible Church, Nashville Central

Karen and Crawford have given us all a vision for marriage to be both a "sacred conduit" and an "inviting portrait" of God Himself along with His plans and purposes. Learn of how God's legacy of faithfulness was woven in their marriage from both challenges and the character of a former slave named Peter. This book will give you practical tips, engaging stories but, most of all, hope for your journey in marriage.

JACK ALEXANDER
Chairman of The Reimagine Group
Author of *The God Impulse: The Power of Mercy in an Unmerciful World*

My marriage is thriving because of the example they lived out in front of me. I'm excited for you to glean from these pages what I was taught firsthand.

HOLLY LORITTS GIBSON

We have read many, many books on marriage, but this one is really different. Through their own life stories, Karen and Crawford draw out a compelling call to live out godly marriages, not just for today, but for the urgency of shaping future generations we may never see or know. Even after forty-five years of our own Christian marriage, we discovered many fresh insights and new thoughts to better live out our own sacred covenant.

BUCK AND SUSAN MCCABE
Retired Executive VP, Chick-fil-A, Inc.

Crawford and Karen have been blessed with almost a half-century of marriage and have certainly built into their children a wonderful missional legacy that embodies Deuteronomy 6:4–7. They show that the best way to be a good parent is to have a loving marriage.

BRYANT WRIGHT
Senior Pastor, Johnson Ferry Baptist Church

For forty-seven years Crawford and Karen have lived such an inspiring model of marriage that all four of their children asked their father to officiate their weddings. With that credibility they share a compelling and realistic game plan for a successful and significant marriage. This is a must-read for the soon-to-be married as well as the already-married couple.

STEVE REINEMUND
Executive in Residence at Wake Forest University

Crawford and Karen speak with admirable candor and integrity of their own years of marriage. It's hard to get across such testimony in a way that's just right—not too much information, but also not so circumspect you wonder what the author is hiding. But here their personal stories (and Crawford and Karen spring from very different backgrounds) are engagingly interwoven with the rest of the book, and the family stories that illustrate the main points are suffused with good humor, humility, and frequent self-deprecation. Moreover, the book is wonderfully and deeply God-centered. Though the authors protest that this is not a book on the theology of marriage, it displays more and better theology on this subject than some books that purport to focus on theology.

D. A. CARSON
Research Professor of New Testament, Trinity Evangelical Divinity School

Dianne and I have had the privilege of knowing and having a great friendship with he and Karen for over thirty years. I have heard Crawford teach, preach, challenge and mentor from consistently one perspective . . . what does God's Word say about the topic? I have experienced his wisdom and clarity of message, all spoken in love and humility in arenas, pulpits, boardrooms, and around a meal. This newest book by him and Karen is no exception to their consistent past. I know you will be challenged and encouraged by it, because you can trust the Source and the messenger.

STEVE ROBINSON
Retired Executive VP, Chick-fil-A, Inc.

Your Marriage Today . . . and Tomorrow is a gem. Written by one of America's most sought-after teaching couples, it addresses a large need in marriage literature. It is straightforward, yet eloquent; compact, yet expansive; realistic, yet filled with hope. Whether you are newly married, seeking to grow a mature marriage, or want to leave a solid generational legacy, this warm, winsome book will provide lifelong guidance and inspiration for you and your spouse. It is already impacting Wendy and me in just that way!

JOHN D. BECKETT
Chairman, The Beckett Companies; author of *Loving Monday and Mastering Monday*

YOUR MARRIAGE TODAY

...AND TOMORROW

MAKING YOUR RELATIONSHIP MATTER NOW
AND FOR GENERATIONS TO COME

CRAWFORD & KAREN LORITTS

MOODY PUBLISHERS

CHICAGO

Edited by Elizabeth Cody Newenhuyse
Cover design: Smartt Guys design
Interior design: Smartt Guys design
Authors photo: William Rainey

Library of Congress Cataloging-in-Publication Data

Names: Loritts, Crawford W., author.
Title: Your marriage today ... and tomorrow : making your relationship matter
   now and for generations to come / Crawford Loritts and Karen Loritts.
Description: Chicago : Moody Publishers, 2018.
Identifiers: LCCN 2018008732 (print) | LCCN 2018015418 (ebook) | ISBN
   9780802496584 (ebook) | ISBN 9780802418159
Subjects: LCSH: Marriage--Religious aspects--Christianity.
Classification: LCC BV835 (ebook) | LCC BV835 .L67 2018 (print) | DDC
   248.8/44--dc23
LC record available at https://lccn.loc.gov/2018008732

ISBN: 978-0-8024-1815-9

We hope you enjoy this book from Moody Publishers. Our goal is to provide high-quality, thought-provoking books and products that connect truth to your real needs and challenges. For more information on other books and products that will help you with all your important relationships, go to www.moodypublishers.com or write to:

Moody Publishers
820 N. La Salle Boulevard
Chicago, IL 60610

1 3 5 7 9 10 8 6 4 2

Printed in the United States of America

To Our Grandchildren:

Quentin, Myles, Jaden, Jaxon, Ashlyn, Leilani, Bryana, Sinaiya, Addison, Harrison, and Hendrix.

Praying that God will bless you with strong, godly marriages and families. Trusting God that you will walk faithfully with Him and treasure, nurture, and pass on what has been placed in your hands. God, do it we pray . . .

Love,

PAPA AND MIMI LORITTS
Psalm 78:5–7

Contents

Foreword

I have never met a couple who married hoping to make each other miserable. But time and again I have sat in my office, listening to the pain of a couple who were, indeed, miserable in their marriage. What happens between the "I do" and "I won't"?

One of the great tragedies of modern Western culture is that so many couples fail to discover the path to a loving, caring, supportive relationship. What they desired so deeply has become elusive.

On the other hand, there are many couples that have found marriage to be deeply satisfying. They are each committed to the well-being of the other. They know the truth of the ancient Hebrew saying, "Two are better than one." Crawford and Karen Loritts are among those who have been blessed with this kind of marriage.

They will be the first to admit that it has been a journey. As you will discover, their backgrounds are extremely different. The sociologists may well have put them in the category of "least likely to succeed." However, one unifying factor provided the glue that held them together long enough to discover God's plan for marriage: their personal faith and commitment to Jesus Christ.

The God who instituted marriage also gave us principles by which we are to relate to each other as husband and wife. The attitude of love is the foundation upon which we build. It was demonstrated by Christ Himself, who humbled Himself to becoming a man so that He could pay the ultimate sacrifice for our sins. When we allow His Spirit to rule in our hearts, we too learn how to truly love and serve each other. Two lovers will have a great marriage. This is not a book of platitudes. You will hear the voices of a couple who are willing to share their ups and downs, their failures and successes. They are looking back on their lives together and drawing from the well of experience in order to help younger couples discover the marriage they dreamed of having when they got married.

One thread that runs through the book is the reality that your marriage is not only about you but about your children, grandchildren, and generations to come. It impacts not only your family, but other families, the church, and God's eternal mission. Your marriage is designed to be a living expression of what happens when couples live according to God's plans. A God-guided marriage will have an eternal impact.

As you read this book, it is my prayer that you will hear the still, small voice of God whisper hope and direction into your marriage. One small step at a time, you can have the marriage that God intended and you desired. The questions at the end of each chapter will help you take those steps toward the marriage you've always wanted.

Gary D. Chapman, PhD
Author of *The 5 Love Languages®:The Secret to Love That Lasts*

Introduction

Some time ago John Hinkley with Moody Publishers asked Karen and me to consider writing a book on marriage. As Karen and I discussed the possibility, we wondered what we could say that has not already been put in print. After all, there are so many wonderful resources—books, conferences, radio programs, and much more—on marriage and family readily available and accessible to just about all of us. Yet, as Karen and I prayed and discussed the possibility, we felt that we should put in print what we believe and feel deeply about marriage.

Karen and I have been married now for forty-seven years. We have four adult children and eleven grandchildren. For more than thirty years we have spoken, written, and shared in various forums and interviews our hopes, concerns, and some of the lessons we have learned along the way about the beauty and gift of marriage. But when you hear us speak, you will sense hovering behind our message a desire to share the missional, legacy aspect of marriage. In other words, we stress that marriage is not just about now, today, but it shapes and affects the future. That is what this book is about. We now sense that the time is right to share more broadly what we feel so deeply.

Although this is not a book on the theology of marriage, what we say is anchored in the Scriptures. God's Word is transformative and enduring. It not only gives us the sacred "why" for marriage, it also provides us with the guidelines, hope, and power to experience what God intended for every marriage and family both for today and tomorrow. Therefore, we believe it is very important that what we say is seen in the context and through the lens of the Word of God.

As you read this book, we are praying that your heart will be filled with hope and encouragement, that you will experience a sense of purpose and mission in your marriage. We are praying that even though as a couple you may come from very different backgrounds, you will know and experience the wonderful grace and power of God producing sweet oneness in your marriage. We are praying that you will catch a vision as to how God can use your marriage to point others to Christ. We are praying that the fruit of your commitment to God and to your marriage will give your children and those you influence a solid foundation to build strong, godly marriages and families during their moment in history. God, please do this, we pray.

Just a word about our approach to writing the book. Karen and I have coauthored this book. However, rather than Karen writing a chapter and then I write a chapter, or writing it in such a way that we alternate our insights, we decided to write it with one voice. This seems to work best for us. Although you will see the pronoun "I," it represents "us." The content of this book has been shaped by both of us and is the product of sharing our lives together for more than forty-seven years.

We are so grateful to God for our partnership with Moody Publishers. We couldn't ask for a better team to work with. Thank you, John Hinkley, Betsey Newenhuyse, and all those involved in making this message a reality. It has been a joy and blessing to team up with you.

A special thanks to Jim Jenks, my executive assistant, who helps me to navigate through the details of my ministry and carve out the time to write. Jim, your friendship and serving spirit is a joy to my soul.

We want to thank Fellowship Bible Church, where I have the privilege of serving as senior pastor, for giving us the opportunity to serve and minister to marriages and families. We are grateful for the churches, conferences, and various ministries who, through the years, extended opportunities for Karen and me to share much of what we have written about in this book. We especially want to thank Dennis and Barbara Rainey, the cofounders of FamilyLife. They are dear friends, and we have enjoyed a partnership in ministry for more than thirty years. Thank you, Dennis and Barbara, for your friendship, encouragement, and the opportunity to both express and shape what we see and feel about marriage and the family.

We want to thank our children, Bryan, Heather, Bryndan, and Holly. Mom and I are blessed beyond measure, and our hearts are filled with praise to our great God for the joy and privilege of being your parents. As we watch how you are handling the opportunities, challenges, and responsibilities of nurturing your marriages and shaping the next generation, we are profoundly grateful for the grace of God. In large part, it is because of you that we have written this book. Thank you . . .

The Vision and the Mission

Crawford: May 22, 1971 stands as the happiest day of my life. Why wouldn't it be? After all, I said "I do" to the love of my life, and our hearts were filled with hope, dreams, and the anticipation of a wonderful future and life together. But I was also sobered by this incredible sense of responsibility. As I glanced at my parents sitting on the front row, my heart was filled with gratitude to God for the example and model of love and commitment to their marriage and to each other. I remember thinking, "Oh God, help Karen and me to have the same thing."

Then after the ceremony, Pop whispered in my ear, "C. W., remember, you asked to marry Karen. Whatever it takes, you make sure you take care of her in every way."

I must admit the old boy put the fear of God in me. But that wasn't his intention. He was reminding me that next to my relationship with Christ, I had just made the most important commitment of my life.

Our wedding was beautiful. All weddings are beautiful. As a pastor, I love doing weddings. But it is easy to get caught up in the ceremony, the celebration, and all the trappings of the big day, and forget the reality that a *marriage—the* foundation of civilization—is taking place.

Karen and I have four children, and I have been privileged to perform their wedding ceremonies. When each of our children came to me and said that they were in a serious relationship and considering getting married, I reminded them—like Pop reminded me—that next to surrendering their lives to Christ, this was the most important decision they will ever make.

Important for each other, yes. But there's more to marriage than the bride and groom. Marriage is about now and the future. No, not just the future as in our lifetime, but the future as in affecting future generations. So when a couple stands before a minister, surrounded by witnesses, they are making a commitment that will set the course and trajectory of their lives, that will impact a time that they cannot see but will influence. The shape and condition of their marriage will be seen, felt, and experienced by the couple's children. It will profoundly affect those children's outlook and approach to marriage and how they imprint *their* children. And so on . . .

But *how* does marriage affect future generations, for better or for worse? How can we pass on a godly legacy to those who come after us? What is God's vision for marriage—and the mission He has charged us with?

The Bible answers these questions. In fact, God through His Word is clear about the vision and mission of marriage. Regrettably, we've allowed the influences in the culture and society to cloud this vision, redefine marriage, and repackage how we think about this sacred institution. Satan, the enemy of God and His purposes, wants to either destroy marriage or keep every couple confused about God's plan for their marriage. Why? *Because marriage is the sacred conduit by which God's plan and purposes are passed on from one generation to the next.*

Marriage: The First Institution

In this book we'll be sharing a lot about how this has worked (or hasn't worked) in our families and family histories. But before we share our stories, we want to start with God's story—His Word. So let's go all the way back to the beginning to see what God had in mind.

Now, you're not going to see the words "marriage" or "family" in this passage from Genesis, which talks about God's intentions for creating us. However, God's plan for marriage and family and our stewardship responsibility—that is, what we do with what God has given us—are anchored to this text. Look closely at these words:

Then God said, "Let us make man in our image, after our likeness. And let them have dominion over the fish of the sea and over the birds of the heavens and over the livestock and over all the earth and over every creeping thing that creeps on the earth."

So God created man in his own image,
in the image of God he created him;
male and female he created them.

And God blessed them. And God said to them, "Be fruitful and multiply and fill the earth and subdue it, and have dominion over the fish of the sea and over the birds of the heavens and over every living thing that moves on the earth." (Gen. 1:26–28)

In His image

There are several points I want to highlight from the passage. One, since we were made in the image of God, it follows that as a couple we are to reflect and steward that image. You can see that the word *image* is used three times in these verses. God wants it understood that we were created to not only be in relationship with Him but to *look* like Him. We are to reflect and magnify the character and nature of our great God. What's most important in the marriage is what the marriage says about God and not what it says about us. God is the object, essence, and focus of the marriage and our life together as a couple. This indeed is what and who we live for and what we place in the hands of the next generation. His image won't fade away. Ours will.

Karen and I have eleven grandchildren. We absolutely love spending time with them and making wonderful memories together. Vacations, calls, FaceTime, special events, surprise visits, texts, and more are intentional ways in which we build memories and stay connected. What great times we have and share together. But we also know that these memories and expressions of our love are not ultimately enduring. Time marches on. The day will come when they will no longer hear Mimi and Papa's voices. Hopefully they will tell their children about us and the memories of vacations at the beach or the hours we spent laughing and being silly. But this too will eventually fade.

> What's most important in the marriage is what the marriage says about God and not what it says about us.

What will last? What will have mattered most? What will give them hope? The image of God. If our marriage and approach to parenting and grandparenting have reflected the character and nature of our great God, and if our journey through this life has been the story of God's faithfulness and supernatural intervention on our behalf, then by God's grace we have benchmarked their pilgrimage and given them that which lasts forever. This is the mission of marriage.

In addition, there's a very important pronoun in verse 26, the opening line of the passage: "Let *us* make man in *our* image" (emphasis added). God is speaking, but the pronouns are plural. He didn't say, "Let *me* make man in *my* image." No, He said "us" and "our." This is not only a clear reference to the involvement of the Trinity in our creation, but it also refers to how the image of God is to be shared and experienced. The plural pronouns give us a window into the relationship that God the Father, God the Son, and God the Holy Spirit have with one another and, thus, the relationship we are to have with them and with other human beings, especially in the context of marriage and the family.

Further, the verse says that we were made in their "image" and in their "likeness." What does this mean? As I mentioned, it clearly is a reference to the character and nature of God, but I also believe that it means something more. Although it is not explicitly stated, this is a hint toward and a window into the unity and oneness experienced by the Trinity. To be made in their image and to be made into their likeness is to be created for relationship and community with God and with one another. We are created to be loved and to love.

Marriage and family are intended to be a reflection and portrait of the oneness and love found in the Trinity. Just as God created us to experience that love and unity, He has called us to *become* and model that love and unity. The joy and purity of this love is compelling and attractive, coming from the heart of the Trinity and fulfilled in community and relationship with others, especially in marriage. This too is a reflection of the image of God.

Not alone

Further, marriage is *designed to meet our aloneness needs.* Look at these words in Genesis 2:18: "Then the LORD God said, 'It is not good that man should be alone; I will make him a helper fit for him.'" Up until this point everything that God created is followed by the declaration, "it was good." Now He creates Adam and says that it is not good that he should be alone. God didn't say that the creation of Adam was not good. He said that the fact that "the man" was alone was not good.

God deliberately created Adam with a need that God Himself chose not to directly meet. He created Adam with the need for a companion. It is important to note that this need in Adam was not because he had sinned and therefore was the consequence of missing the mark or disobedience. That would come later. God makes this declaration before Adam sinned.

God intentionally built into Adam a need to be with another— a need not to be alone, a need He could fulfill by designing another human being to meet that need. In so doing, together Adam and Eve would experience and reflect the image of God and know and represent the love and community experienced and enjoyed by the Trinity.

In Genesis 2:19–23, God gives Adam the assignment of naming the animals, and thereby underscores to Adam his need for a companion. Verse 20 says, "But for Adam there was not found a helper fit for him." Adam then falls asleep, and God takes a rib from his side and creates Eve. When Adam wakes up he is greeted with an unimaginable gift. God presents Eve to Adam.

Adam is ecstatic! Look at what he says: "This at last is bone of my bones and flesh of my flesh; she shall be called Woman, because she was taken out of Man" (Gen. 2:23). In so many words, Adam says, "Wow! I can't believe my eyes . . . She is from me and for me." They were together. Adam was no longer alone.

Karen and I met at the beginning of my sophomore year in college. We began spending a lot of time together. We took long walks and would talk for hours. I couldn't stop thinking about her and I didn't want to stop thinking about her. Something was happening to me. She was experiencing the same thing. We were in love, and our love for each other was growing. That summer I went on tour with the college quartet. Those guys were great friends and we liked hanging out together. In fact, we were together constantly. But I was lonely. I missed Karen. I just couldn't see myself without her. And it was reassuring to know that she felt the same about me. God designed us to meet each other's aloneness needs. She is God's amazing gift to me.

Leave, hold fast, become one

After Adam jubilantly welcomes Eve, God seals the deal by commissioning the institution of marriage in Genesis 2:24. "Therefore shall a man *leave* his father and his mother and *hold fast* to his wife, and they shall *become one flesh*" (emphasis added). This verse highlights the new reality that every healthy marriage must embrace. Every wedding ceremony I perform, I spend time explaining this foundational reality.

Most marriages that fall apart—or just atrophy—do so because of failure to pursue the three crucial choices outlined in this verse: "Leave." "Hold fast." "Become one flesh." Let's look at each of these.

First, *leave*. This does not mean to abandon your parents or no longer have a loving, healthy relationship with them. Being married doesn't mean that we replace our relationship with our parents. It means that the relationship of necessity changes. To leave means to establish healthy independence as a couple. When we get married, we are to take care of ourselves—to physically, financially, and emotionally leave home and the care of our parents and establish and embrace our new identity as a married couple. We choose to own our choices and decisions, along with the consequences of those decisions.

There may be seasons in a marriage in which you need assistance from your parents, but this help should always be received as an adult and not as a dependent child. There should be a spirit of gratitude and not entitlement. Offer to pay back money lent to you. If you have to stay with your parents, set a date when you will leave, and make sure that you contribute to the household. Don't complain about your spouse to your parents or invite them into your conflicts and disagreements. Keep in mind that overdependence on parents will rob you of the strength you need as a couple to greet your future and forge your legacy.

> Keep in mind that overdependence on parents will rob you of the strength you need as a couple to greet your future and forge your legacy.

Sometimes it's the parents who have a hard time letting their married children leave. They offer unsolicited advice, they're quick to criticize decisions and even get angry and pout when the couple doesn't spend as much time with them as they would like. But leaving is healthy and necessary for the marriage to thrive.

Second, *hold fast*. This expression comes from a Hebrew word that means to "stick" or to "attach." But this is something we must *choose* to do. Marriage does not take place in a protected environment, cocooned from the forces of the world. The commitment and vows made on your wedding day will be tested and attacked.

Think about it. Every marriage brings together two sinful people who come with baggage. Couple this with a culture and environment that doesn't exactly give a standing ovation for the biblical framework for marriage and, by the way, Satan's desire to derail and destroy marriage and family. When we say, "I do," we have to buckle our seat belts and determine to hold fast.

Holding fast to each other means that you have made the decision that no relationship on earth is more important than the relationship you have with each other as a couple. So we are to be vigilant and intentional in maintaining and protecting this core priority. Our children, parents, extended family, careers, and other interests that we feel passionate about should not take the place of the heart focus we have for each other in the marriage.

So many marriages fall apart because the relationship has been taken for granted, and couples are drawn toward other affections. Like the boat that is not secured to the dock, our default is to drift.

Holding fast also means to embrace mutual interdependence. This is not to be confused with an unhealthy codependence, which is a dysfunctional, excessive reliance on other people for approval and a sense of identity. But to be married is a declaration of need. We got married not because we wanted a roommate or we wanted someone to propel us toward success. No, we got married because we could not live without that person. They met our aloneness need. They completed us.

This is healthy need, and holding fast declares that we continue to need each other. This need wasn't met when we sealed the deal on the wedding day; it is an ongoing need for the warmth, love, and attention

To be married is a declaration of need.

of the person we committed our lives to. We need to love and to be loved.

Stubborn independence is an expression of pride and will erect a wall between you and your marriage partner. To embrace our need for each other is an expression of humility that breaks down barriers in the relationship. This too is what it means to hold fast to each other.

Holding fast means mutual protection. Love covers and intentionally protects the one loved from exposure to danger and harm. It's not like the guy I saw on the news who was sitting in the stands next to his wife at a baseball game. A foul ball was heading their way and he ducked, but she got hit in the head. I bet she had a few things to say to him. Like, "Mr. Protector, why didn't you try to catch the ball or at least shield me from getting hit?"

To be married means, as the saying goes, that we have each other's backs. We will defend and fight for safety, protection, and the well-being of our marriage partner. We will take the hit in order to protect them. This means we will not knowingly allow anyone, including our children and parents or extended family, to trespass boundaries and to hurt the one we have committed our lives to.

Third, *become one flesh*. Adam and Eve celebrated their commitment to each other through sexual intercourse. And indeed, this was pure, guiltless celebration. Look at Genesis 2:25: "And the man and his wife were both naked and were not ashamed." No shame. Further, their sexual intimacy affirmed the message that they were one and committed to each other for the rest of their lives. Sex is the sign and seal of commitment and oneness in marriage.

True, soul-enriching intimacy takes time and tested commitment.

As important as sex is in a healthy marriage, intimacy ("become one flesh") means so much more. Intimacy is a journey to be embraced. This is suggested by the expression "*shall* become one flesh" (emphasis added). Intimacy is an ongoing, growing knowing of each other. We are intimate and we are *becoming* intimate.

Over time our identities become so delightfully intertwined that we know and feel how the other person thinks and how they will respond. Our communication goes beyond words—a look, a glance, a touch says it all. This kind of intimacy has been built on trust and the exclusive pursuit of each other through the years. Love and passion come early on, but true, soul-enriching intimacy takes time and tested commitment. Acceptance has been chosen over rejection. The gift of forgiveness has washed away resentment. There is safety and the comfort of knowing that there is one person in the world who is committed to knowing me and yet loves me unconditionally. No performance necessary. Intimacy.

But remember, intimacy is a choice. We must be determined to pursue this ongoing, growing knowing of each other.

What Jesus Does

Intimacy, as important as it is, primarily is about us. But, as we have seen, marriage is also about mission, modeling, and passing on the image of our great God from one generation to the next. Marriage, as the first institution, is intended to be the incarnation of God's plan and purposes for all of human history. Now I fully realize that thought was probably nowhere near our minds on our wedding day. But you can be assured it is front and center in God's mind.

Of course, we know that God's beautiful creation is marred by sin. When Adam and Eve sinned, everything about them was damaged, including their relationship with each other (Gen. 3). Guiltless peace and transparency were replaced with shame and secrecy. They covered themselves with leaves. They attempted to hide themselves from God in order to escape accountability for their disobedience. They passed blame on each other. But God indeed held them responsible and accountable for their sinful disobedience.

The damage had been done. Sin had blasted its way into human history and from this first couple forward we have been left reeling from the devastation of the impact of sin. Marriage, originally designed to reflect and steward the image of God from one generation to the next, now is contaminated. Competition and selfishness erode unity, and self-preservation dwarfs loving sacrifice. Through Adam and Eve's disobedience, the devil sought to damage and derail marriage and its mission.

But thank God for Jesus! God, through Christ, has paid the penalty for our sin, and through faith in Him, we have been restored to fellowship with God the Father and given the joy and privilege to live on mission for and with Him. This means that we are forgiven and empowered to be and do what God designed. Couples that are surrendered to the lordship of Christ have marriages that have been realigned to God's purposes and plan for marriage.

This is the message or statement that marriage is to make. Every marriage is to be a statement about the redemption, honor, and glory of our great Savior, Jesus Christ. It is our passion to build our marriage on, about, and through Him. There is no higher goal, dream, or ambition. And when we give ourselves to pursuing this vision, our marriage becomes God's statement to a watching world during our moment in history as well as the breeding ground for hope for future generations.

What will we place in our children's hands? When our children open their presents after their wedding ceremony, hopefully they will smile with the realization that their parents gave them the best gift they could have ever received—a vibrant, Christ-centered marriage.

Karen and I come from completely different backgrounds, but Jesus is our common ground, starting point, and the foundation for our lives and our marriage. Throughout this book, we want to share with you what God has been teaching us about marriage and its influence on future generations. But first, our stories . . .

To think about . . .

"Like the boat that is not secured in the dock, our default is to drift." Are you aware of that tendency in your marriage? How can you prevent that "drift"?

Where We Come From

Crawford: *Our kids laugh about how different Karen's and my backgrounds are. They say that I grew up in a sort of a black version of "Leave It to Beaver," while their mom grew up in very challenging circumstances in the city. They good-naturedly blame certain habits and quirks of ours on our upbringing. For example, Karen is always aware of her surroundings, and as our kids were growing up she would remind them to be aware of what's going on around them and keep an eye on suspicious characters (not a bad idea). They said that this was a carryover of having grown up in some pretty tough neighborhoods.*

But what they also have seen and witnessed is the hope and power of the gospel to take two very different people, transform our lives, and bless us with a tenacious, deep love for each other. It would mark them and give them a vision of the broad, sweeping power of the cross. What He did for their parents He could do for them.

T o say that Karen and I come from different family backgrounds would be an understatement. Before we got married, an older mutual friend advised us to reconsider getting married because our family backgrounds weren't "compatible." Boy, am I glad we didn't listen to that advice. Besides, our backgrounds are not our common ground. The cross, and our mutual pursuit of Christlikeness, is our common ground. More on that later.

For good or bad, we can't do anything about our heritage (where we came from, what's been done to us, and what's been placed in our hands). But we can do something about our legacy (the determined choices and decisions we make during our journey that will give the next generation a foundation of hope and confidence).

But the reality is that so many of us know too well the pain of divorce, rejection, and even abuse. Some of us don't know what a healthy marriage looks like. What we have inherited are examples of failed commitments and fractured relationships. We want to trust ourselves to someone else, but we have no compelling, healthy models of hope to draw from.

Yet no matter where we came from, there *is* hope. The gospel declares that the failures and pain of our past and the failures of those who are closest to us don't have to be our experience or our legacy. Frankly, if God raised a dead Jesus, He can give us a new beginning, a fresh start. We are not the hopeless victims of our past. This means that we don't have to be what has been done to us and what we have seen. The God of the universe, through Christ, can step into our lives, mend and heal our hearts, fill in the missing pieces, and make us models and ambassadors of hope for this and future generations. We can know and experience marriage the way in which it was intended to be and not the distorted, tortured portrait that has been presented to us.

> We don't have to be what has been done to us and what we have seen.

Karen and I know firsthand this transforming grace of God. That's why we want to share our stories with you. Here's mine . . .

Crawford's Story

The patriarch

My father's side of the family is the story of strong, intact marriages. Pop was born in Conover, NC, on February 13, 1914. He was one of fourteen children (seven boys and seven girls) born to my grandparents, Milton and Anna Loritts. Peter, my great-grandfather and Milton's father, was a former slave. Peter lived to a ripe old age, and my father said that one of his most vivid memories of Peter was watching him sit for hours on the front porch of the old house, rocking back and forth in a rocking chair singing hymns and spirituals, and occasionally pausing to pray out loud. He also loved the Bible. As the story goes, because he couldn't read, he would have his children and grandchildren read him the Scriptures.

Peter loved the Lord, and he loved his family. He had a daughter (Georgia) and two sons, my great-uncle Hazy Peter ("H.P.") and my grandfather Milton. Unfortunately, I never had the privilege of knowing any of them personally. They all died before I was born. But I knew and felt the impact of their lives. I remember as a little boy attending family reunions and sitting on the front porch or around the table and listening to my aunts and uncles tell countless stories of Peter and my grandparents. I was mesmerized. Looking back, faith, family, and the church served as common themes or the backdrop to most of the stories. And Peter was the patriarch. It all began with him.

Think about it. Slavery was no idyllic, romantic experience. The institution of slavery destroyed families. We have no record of Peter's mother or father. Chances are, when he became a young teenager, he was sold, or one or both of his parents were sold, were killed, or died. No one ever knew anything about Peter's parents, or if they did, no one shared their story. But we do know that somewhere along the line, he placed his faith in Christ, nurtured his love for the Lord, and developed a passion and commitment to his family. God, through a former slave, forged generations of strong marriages and families.

I have often wondered where Peter's commitment to the family came from. Let's face it: he didn't exactly grow up during a time in which there was a lot of affirmation and commitment to the preservation of black families. So, what was the driving force? Where did this commitment come from? Was it born out of pain and a longing to preserve what he himself desperately wanted but couldn't have? I suppose in large part that was probably the case.

But his passion for the family, perhaps stirred by what he didn't have, was driven and fueled by faith in Christ and shaped by the word of God. We must never underestimate the power of Jesus Christ to change our lives and the trajectory of our future. Jesus changes everything (2 Cor. 5:17). What Peter experienced and where he came from is not what he placed in the hands of future generations of Lorittses. No, he placed in his children's hands who and what he had become, a follower of Jesus Christ. In that regard, he became the portrait of the desired destination of what every generation of Lorittses should do and become.

> **God, through a former slave, forged generations of strong marriages and families.**

And by the grace of God, that vision and mission has marked our family. No, not everyone in the Loritts family tree is or has been a follower of Christ. As the saying goes, God has no grandchildren. But the compelling power of the gospel and the priority and central focus of family has been the anchor theme of our family from 1865 to this very day. Oh God, may it continue!

The greatest man I've ever known

This vision and passion gripped the heart of my grandfather, Milton. He too was a follower of Jesus Christ and was deeply committed to his family. As I said, he and my grandmother had fourteen children and modeled before them a commitment to Christ and a love and commitment to the family. My dad, Crawford Loritts Sr., picked up the mantle and modeled this same vision and mission before us.

To say that my dad had an impact on me is an understatement (I have written about his influence on my life in my book *Never Walk Away*). Next to Jesus Christ, my father is the greatest man I've ever known. No, he wasn't a community leader. He never held public office. He wasn't a member of a profession that brought him visibility and attention. He worked for more than thirty years for an A&P warehouse in Newark, NJ.

What made him great is who he was. He lived for what mattered most. His character, integrity, and commitment to his wife and his children spoke volumes. In fact, Pop was not big on lectures (now, he did have a few stock speeches he would give to me and my sisters when we messed up or he sensed we were headed in the wrong direction). Again, he did and modeled before us what was most important. For example, although he and Mom had a lot of friends, he shied away from doing things that didn't include his family. Every Saturday was family day. He worked nights but would work out his schedule so that he could be at my ball games. We went to church every Sunday. He led our family.

And did he ever love his wife, our mother. The fastest way to get on the wrong side of Pop was to disrespect his wife. As children, we learned early on that it was too expensive to cross that line. One day when I was about sixteen, I had a bit of a mental lapse. Mom asked me a question, which I thought had a very obvious answer. So, in a very disrespectful, smart-alecky tone of voice I said, "That's a dumb question." (As the words were coming out of my mouth, I remember thinking something like, "This is probably not going to end well.") My mother looked at me as if I had lost my mind and said, "Boy, who do you think you're talking to?" (Now, I knew where this was heading and the better part of wisdom was not to answer yet another obvious question.) Then she said the words that I dreaded to hear, "I think your father needs to know how you just talked to me." Not good! At this point it was time to cast aside pride and humble myself. Not only did I apologize, I begged Mom not to tell Pop. I was sweating bullets. I guess she thought my repentance was sincere. She never told him.

> The fastest way to get on the wrong side of Pop was to disrespect his wife.

Like all of us, my parents didn't have a perfect marriage. They had their share of disagreements and areas in which they needed to grow. But they had a commitment to the Lord and to each other, and they took their marriage vows seriously. They loved each other. They were committed to each other. They protected each other. You thought of them as a unit. It wasn't just Crawford or just Sylvia. It was Crawford and Sylvia or Sylvia and Crawford. What a sweet picture of oneness. What a treasure.

Faith, family, community

Unlike Pop, Mom didn't come from a background of strong marriages. She was the oldest and had a brother and a sister. Mom, Uncle Henry, and Aunt Margaret had different fathers. My mother never knew who her father was. My grandmother, Janie Grey, raised them by herself. So, they grew up in a single-parent household, raised by a mother who worked as a domestic and barely got by. This was not exactly the breeding ground for future strong marriages and intact families.

I remember asking Mom some years ago why she wasn't a statistic and how did she develop such a heart and commitment to her marriage and family? After all, the odds were not in her favor. Think about it. You don't know who your father is and there aren't a lot of resources to help you. It seems to me that the pull toward becoming what you see and experience would be irresistible. In fact, all of the studies and statistics tell us that it's pretty normal. So, I wanted to know what made things different for my mother.

I'll never forget what she said to me. She said because they didn't have a father and a husband in the house didn't mean that they were without compelling role models and examples of marriage and family in their tight-knit community. She grew up in the South during the days of overt segregation and Jim Crow. This meant that the black community had to care for and nurture its own. Further, she said that the church and neighbors filled in the gaps and helped to give her positive expectations. They gave her a sense of hope and confidence and affirmed her dignity as one who bears the image of God.

> I remember asking Mom some years ago why she wasn't a statistic.

More importantly, she surrendered her heart and life to Jesus Christ at an early age. She fell in love with the Lord and with the Word of God. Jesus Christ made all things new for Sylvia Grey and placed in her heart the faith to believe that she could have a husband who loved her and a family that they could raise to know and walk with the Lord. You see, Mom's vision and passion for marriage and family was not borrowed from my dad. No, it was the work of the cross and the transforming power of the gospel. Yes, Mom and Pop came from different backgrounds, but their common ground was the cross.

Like Pop, family was the core priority of Sylvia Loritts. I can't begin to describe the sense of security this gave to my sisters and me. When you grow up in a household where you knew and experienced love and acceptance, and you saw a mother and father who loved, valued, and respected each other, it gives you hope and confidence that you can do and experience the same. I saw what they did and the decisions they made. Their example placed in me a desire to be married and to have children so that I could do the same for them. Again, I don't remember lengthy conversations with either my mother or my father about how to be a good husband or a father. They lived it. What a gift.

Karen's Story

A generational cycle

Karen adored her grandparents, Harvey and Jennie Williams. They were born and raised in Philadelphia, PA. Both were teenagers when they got married, and they had three children in five years, two daughters and a son. Her mother, Marlene, was the youngest.

Karen's grandfather was a good provider, working long, hard

hours. He made time for his children, taking them on trips to the New Jersey shore and putting together block parties in the neighborhood. Karen's grandmother worked for the local school system while juggling her duties as a wife and mother. Young Marlene was the pride and joy of her father. He loved each of his children but gave special attention to his youngest daughter, giving her just about everything she asked for.

Over time, however, the pressures of life began to take a toll on Harvey and Jennie. Although their love and commitment to their two daughters and son never wavered, their marriage began to deteriorate. As a very young couple, they were unprepared for what life was hurling at them. Sadly, the marriage ended.

No one knows the specific reason(s) for the divorce. But what is apparent is that their marriage mirrored a generational cycle of young love, marriage, parenthood, and separation or divorce. Marlene took the breakup of the marriage the hardest. Her hurt was turned to anger, and she blamed her mother for the divorce.

Marlene was a very intelligent, beautiful woman. When she graduated from high school, she had opportunities for further education, including vocational training—but life got in the way.

Outwardly she appeared to be filled with confidence. But beneath the surface she was lonely and hurting. She had a hole in her heart. The one relationship that she had treasured, enjoyed, and wanted the most had moved out of the house. She desperately wanted her father back in the home. It hurt deeply. Karen believes that the hurt and longing drew her mother to a series of loveless relationships.

Less than a year after Marlene graduated from high school, she met a young Navy sailor who was home on leave. She became pregnant. Due to complications related to poor prenatal care, Karen arrived four weeks early. It would be years before Karen met her father—a relationship she longed for.

Society labeled her illegitimate, a cruel stigma that would haunt her for years. The first twenty-eight days of her life were spent in the neonatal critical care unit of a city hospital that served the under-resourced and uninsured. She came home to live with her mother and grandmother. In the early years of Karen's life, she and her mom lived in public housing after living with with her grandmother and aunt at times. When she was three, her brother Arthur was born.

The women in Karen's family are smart and resourceful, and Marlene was no exception. She was able to land better-paying jobs, which allowed her to find (a bit) better housing in (somewhat) safer areas of the city for her children. In addition, they knew and experienced the love, care, and protection of extended family members, especially during dark, difficult times.

A lonely girl finds church

Then there came a break, a turning point for their family. Karen's mom got a job working for a small business in the neighborhood. The owner, a widower, took notice of this attractive, hardworking single mom. They began a relationship, and he asked her to marry him. She accepted. He was much older than Marlene—thirty-six years older.

Despite that age gap, some things improved for the family. They moved out of the ghetto to a large, beautiful home in a middle-class section of the city. Finally, they enjoyed a sense of security. They were no longer living hand to mouth, barely getting by.

Soon Karen had another little brother. He was the darling of his aged father and youthful mother. They were now a family of five, and life was good.

Karen was nine when her little brother was born. She loved being a big sister. However, with her mom's long hours at work, Karen also inherited the role of "second mother." She didn't have much of a childhood. In addition, their family rarely sat down together for a meal or engaged in family conversation. She points out that they were nothing like her favorite TV show, "Leave It to Beaver." They were three children with two working adults living in a large, comfortable house on a tree-lined street. Yet Karen was lonely and unhappy. She longed for something.

The pastor of a large church lived in their neighborhood, and Karen's mom thought it would be a good thing for Karen and her brother Arthur to start attending church. She sent them, but she didn't go. In fact, until this point, Karen doesn't recall her mother attending church or even mentioning church. Oddly enough, though, Karen was excited about this new experience.

So here you have it. This preteen with her younger brother tagging along shows up for Sunday school. She was directed to a class taught by Ms. Green. Karen loved her class and especially her teacher. Karen remembers how Ms. Green made Bible stories come alive—stories she had never heard before. She looked forward to Sunday so she could hear more Bible stories and be around her teacher. Every Sunday Karen would get a reassuring look and hug from Ms. Green. She gave Karen her first Bible. She cared for each student in a way that sparked a longing in Karen to have what she possessed.

But back at home, things were not going well. Her mother and stepfather were not getting along, and it was stirring up tension in the home. For preteen Karen, the pressures of being the childcare provider, the burden of doing the household chores, and general feelings of unhappiness caused her to entertain thoughts of running away and even suicide. She longed to hear words of appreciation and acceptance from her mother for all that she was doing.

After a few months of attending the large neighborhood church, Karen decided to try another church. There was a smaller church not far from where they lived. The lonely young girl was drawn to the church's big red double doors and stained-glass windows. When she walked inside, she discovered that it was a white congregation. The older pastor and his wife were from Ukraine. His name was Peter Kowalchuk—everybody called him Pastor K. This dear couple warmly welcomed Karen and her brother Arthur with hearty handshakes and bearlike hugs. The children stuck out like a sprinkling of pepper on a sheet of white paper. Yet they were loved, cared for, and included in this small congregation that refused to leave the ethnically changing community. Karen and Arthur had found a church family.

She loved her church. She attended Sunday school and the worship services, became a part of the youth group, and sang in the youth choir. During the summer the church provided scholarships so Karen and Arthur could attend a Bible camp in the Pocono Mountains of Pennsylvania. God used those times at camp to speak deeply to Karen's heart. She cried when it came time to go home. When she was at church she knew comfort and peace. The loneliness was gone.

During her freshman year in high school, Pastor K took the youth group to a concert in downtown Philadelphia. At the end

of the concert, someone gave a message on
John 3:16. It was as if Karen was the only
person in the room and God was speaking
through this man directly to her. God's love
and Jesus sacrificing His life on the Cross
gripped her heart. When the speaker invited
those who wanted to place their faith in
Christ to come forward, Karen was one of

They were loved, cared for, and included in this small congregation that refused to leave the changing community.

the first to respond. One of the counselors shared with her how
she could have a personal relationship with Christ. Karen prayed,
expressing her faith in Christ. That evening she became a part of
the family of God.

God placed in her heart wonderful joy and peace. He also surrounded her with people who loved her and were committed to
helping her be all that God wanted her to be and experience all
that God had in store for her. Pastor K and several of her Sunday-
school teachers discipled her formally and informally. They invited
her into their homes, where she saw models of godly marriages.
Two childless couples especially impacted her life—Pastor and Mrs.
K and Mr. and Mrs. Bourne. Two older single women, Betty Nich-
ols and Mary Entwistle, poured into her life and provided her examples of true womanhood.

When Jesus changed everything

Unfortunately, her mother's marriage continued to deteriorate. Things came to a head during Karen's freshman year in college. Her mother and stepfather had separated a few times and
finally divorced. The cycle of divorce in her family had claimed another victim. First, her grandmother, then her aunt, and now her

mother. Karen remembers this stirring in her a desire, a determination for this not to be her story. God used these events to bring about a milestone commitment in her life. One evening, she knelt beside her bed and placed her life in the Lord's hands to do whatever He wanted with all the details of her life, including marriage.

It was shortly after that commitment God brought our paths together. Jesus Christ changed everything for Karen. He intercepted her life. In His sovereign love and care, He guided a ten-year-old girl to the family of God. Drew her to the cross. Placed in her life people who loved her and modeled before her what God could do and what she could become. Her point of reference was no longer where she came from but her new life in Christ. The tears trickle down my cheeks when I see what our great God has done in and through her life and the gift and blessing she is not only to our family but also to other women, especially young wives and mothers. Karen Loritts is not only the love of my life, she is my hero.

As in the case of my mother, Karen's commitment to marriage and the family was not shaped and informed by her background or family experience. Neither was it borrowed from me or from my background. It is anchored in the cross, informed by the Word of God and encouraged and nurtured by godly women and men who loved her and cared for her soul. This has produced in her a passion for marriage and family.

Choices, Decisions, Commitments

The sobering truth is just because someone comes from a wonderful, godly family is no guarantee that they will have a strong marriage and a thriving family. I have witnessed firsthand the failure of marriages of young couples that come from great families. You're left scratching your head and wondering, "How did this happen?" You would think that their background and exposure would give them a leg up and a desire to replicate what they have seen and experienced. And for the most part, it does.

But choices and decisions are not hereditary. For example, parents homeschool their children or place them in Christian school. For the most part, they conform to or comply with expectations. Then they go off to college and their behavior is inconsistent with what they have seen and heard at home and the environment and context in which they grew up. Did their parents fail them? Were they unprepared? Was there something missing in their development? Maybe. But it could be that they were given what they needed—but didn't *own* what they were given.

Choices. Decisions. The will to respond to God and to do what is right cannot be injected into the veins of the next generation.

What's more, powerful forces are at work to destroy the institution of marriage. The Bible identifies these forces as *the world, the flesh, and the devil*. These forces are powerful and almost irresistible. They were at work through the institution of slavery, which could have fragmented—if not eradicated—our family. They were at work in an attempt to marginalize Sylvia Grey and to lower her expectations and to take hope off the table. They were at work to discourage and victimize a young girl from inner-city Philadelphia. But they didn't succeed.

In the case of my great-grandfather, my mother, and my wife, they encountered and surrendered to the Person who changed everything, Jesus Christ. His love and power changed them and gave them hope and determination to pursue His plans and purposes for their lives, including a marriage and a family that would honor God. They were set free from the bondage of sin and the paralyzing cycle of dysfunction. As they pursued Christ and grew in their relationship with Him they experienced His grace, strength, and sustaining power to keep and live by their marriage vows.

So yes, Karen and I come from very different backgrounds. And along the way, we have had to work through some of those differences and challenges and the general "stuff" that two imperfect people bring to a marriage. But we both have met Jesus and have tasted His power to change us and give us everything we need to have a marriage and family that honors Him. Our common ground is not where we were born or the conditions and circumstances in which we grew up. Our common ground is our love for Jesus Christ, our love and commitment to each other, and our commitment to the biblical covenant and vision for marriage.

> **The will to respond to God and to do what is right cannot be injected into the veins of the next generation.**

The key word is *commitment*. This implies work and sacrifice. To be a follower of Christ does not guarantee you're going to have a godly, thriving marriage. Unfortunately, genuine Christians can have awful marriages. Commitment is not a past experience or a feeling. Commitment implies focused action that underscores the value of the marriage and relationship. It means to pay the price, to give whatever it takes to make the marriage everything God intended for it to be. It means actions that flow out of a heart commitment to prize and protect the relationship. That's what we will look at in the next section.

To think about . . .

Do you relate more to Karen's or Crawford's family background? How have you seen these familial inheritances play out in your own marriage?

Clearly "Mrs. K" and the other adults who poured themselves into young Karen's life paved the way for her loving Jesus and living for Him. Who can you point to in your own life who has similarly influenced you? How could you do the same for others?

The Banks of the River

Karen: *On the eve of the rehearsal dinner for our first son's wedding, I put the finishing touches on an idea for Korie, my soon-to-be daughter-in-law. My desire was to welcome her to our family and symbolically express the intentions of my heart. I had purchased an apron, a heart-shaped pewter box, and some nice stationery. I cut off the pair of apron strings and placed them in the pewter box along with a handwritten note. Here's the essence of what I wrote to our daughter-in-law: "Korie, I make a vow to honor, respect, and support you as God's choice for our son. The Lord blessed us with a precious baby boy to love and nurture to be a man. He once was 'tied' to his mother's apron strings but now I joyfully give you these strings as a symbol of my resolve to keep my vow. Korie, you are the godly daughter-in-love we prayed for since Bryan's birth. May the Lord bless you as you enter this covenant of marriage."*

I n these next chapters, we want to highlight what it takes to protect and nurture a vibrant, missional marriage. We will take a look at the guidelines, habits, and gifts that give life and vibrancy to our marriages and fuel a passion in the next generation to embrace God's heart and vision for marriage.

As we saw in chapter 1, God has a vision, a plan for marriage.

Marriage is meant to "go somewhere"—to arrive at a destination and to declare a message. Specifically, as we said earlier, *marriage is the sacred conduit by which God's plan and purposes are passed on from one generation to the next.* Our children and those close to us are watching and experiencing the impact of how we are stewarding and guarding our marriage and, thus, this sacred mission.

In a way, marriage is like a river. I travel a fair amount, so I am often on airplanes. There's nothing like being thirty thousand feet in the air on a clear, cloudless day. It seems as if you can see forever. An added treat is to be able to see and follow a river as it winds its way to the ocean or to another large body of water. You're drawn in, captured by the movement of the water. You know it has a destination; it's going somewhere. But what keeps it moving in a particular direction? The banks. The route of the river is determined and maintained by the banks. A river with no banks means that we either have a flood or a swamp.

So in our marriages, we intentionally need to make sure that the river is flowing in the right direction. Our marriage is to be the *determined priority* relationship in all of life (Gen. 2:24–25).

But this is not a given. It's not automatic. There are powerful forces at work to wash away or redirect our marriages. We are distracted by so many things. Busyness. Career/work. Materialism. Affairs. Demands/expectations. Children and grandchildren. Selfishness and pride that take every opportunity to mark their territory and drain the life out of the relationship. It's not that we intentionally opened the door and invited "distraction" in. The river just didn't flow in the intended direction. I can't tell you the number of times I've heard couples say, "This is not where we wanted to be . . . We didn't sign up for this."

We have to pay attention to the banks. We all know that it's one thing to look into each other's eyes on our wedding day and declare our vows in the presence of family and friends. But it takes commitment and focused determination to live by those vows and create the environment that protects the marriage from the destructive forces that often, unnoticed at first, pull the relationship off course. We cannot afford to take the banks for granted. In fact, they have to be identified and strengthened.

I met with a couple recently who shared with me that they had been offered a wonderful opportunity to advance their career. This would include nationwide visibility and the opportunity to influence a lot of people. However, along with this platform come expectations and demands. They wanted to know how they could keep their marriage and family a priority and not become another statistic. In other words, they wanted to make sure that the river stayed within the banks. This is the core challenge for every married couple.

As you saw in the last chapter, Karen and I come from very different family backgrounds. Yes, it is true that our common ground is Christ. But we still have had to work through and deal with some of the residue of choices, decisions, and patterns that have affected us. Added to this is that we both have strong personalities and a fair amount of energy. Through the years there were times in which we were not going in the same direction. To mix metaphors, we have had to work on getting on the same page and keeping our marriage within the banks of the river.

How do you keep those "banks" shored up? There are guidelines—"banks"—that we must be aware of, conform to, and practice if our marriage is going to reflect God's plan and purposes for this and future generations and, thus, arrive at its intended destination. We've identified six guidelines.

Building Up Your Banks

1. *Keep your marriage as the core focus of your life but not the central passion of your heart.* Love Jesus more.

When we got married, good resources on marriage and family were scarce. Boy, has that ever changed. During the past thirty years or so, we have seen the development of great resources and ministries committed to building strong marriages and families. There are conferences, books, blogs, radio programs, podcasts, internet resources, and more, geared to help us have healthy, godly homes. What's more, pastors and churches are providing counseling and encouragement for the pre-married, couples, and families. This is great news. We need to do all that we can to encourage couples to know how to keep their marriage and family the core focus of their lives.

But we have a concern.

In our desire to protect the sacred institution of marriage and family, some of us have committed idolatry. We have made our marriages and families an object of worship.

At this point you may be thinking, "Wait a minute, Karen and Crawford! You wrote this book because marriage is the means by which the image of God is passed on from one generation to the next. It is to be the determined priority in life." Yes, this is true. But marriage is meant to honor and glorify God and not to replace Him. Marriage demonstrates the presence and power of Jesus. It does not take His place. The marriage relationship is the channel to both experience and express the glory of God, not to isolate and insulate ourselves from the rest of the world in some protected cocoon.

If the marriage is going to stay within the God-prescribed banks of the river, then our passion to pursue Christ and His plan and purposes for the marriage must be the driving force. In short, our relationship as husband and wife tells the truth about what God cares about and wants to do in and through our union. Marriage was never intended to be an "exception" to Jesus' call to discipleship. It is intended to be Exhibit A for what surrender to the Lordship of Christ looks like.

Jesus said some sobering, strong words in Luke 14:26: "If anyone comes to me and does not *hate* his own father and mother and wife and children and brothers and sisters, yes, and even his own life, he cannot be my disciple" (emphasis added).

This is an astonishing verse. What does Jesus mean by "hate"? Are we to literally hate our family members—including our spouse—in order to be a faithful follower of Christ?

No, I don't think that Jesus is referring to a literal "hate." Rather, I think He is speaking of an incomparable love for Him. He is pointing to Himself as the passion and priority of life. Unless we love Him more than any other relationship in life, including our spouse and children, He says it is impossible to be His disciple. Nothing or no one else is worthy of the love and commitment we're to have for our Savior.

Marriage is intended to be Exhibit A for what surrender to the Lordship of Christ looks like.

It follows, then, that if we love Jesus, we should order our marriage and family around what He is doing. Jesus said in Matthew 6:33, "But seek first the kingdom of God and his righteousness, and all these things will be added to you." We want to bring our marriage and family in line with who Jesus is and how He wants to use our household to advance His kingdom.

To say the least, this is not always easy. It can be a real struggle. Karen and I have been serving together in ministry all of our married lives. Our children have been raised in this context. The nature of what God called us to do required that I travel. So I was away from home a great deal as our kids were growing up. Karen and I loved the Lord, and we were doing what we believed He called us to do. But I can remember many nights crying out to God, asking Him not to allow our children to grow up to be resentful and bitter because I was away. God graciously answered my prayer.

Recently, I read a blog post written by our oldest son, Bryan. Karen and I are humbled by these words. The blog is entitled, "Thanks Dad for not (Always) Showing Up." We want to share it with you because it underscores the priority of Christ and his kingdom.

I'm so thankful my dad didn't come to all of my football, basketball and baseball games. He was thankful too. He never even pretended that perfect attendance at our ball games was a goal, or that his identity was tied into whether or not he showed up. Of course I was excited to see him on occasion standing down the first base line just outside the fence, with his tie loosened cheering me on while I tried to crush the ball. But those days he wasn't there I knew why—he was working. His absences were a real gift to me, a gift I didn't fully appreciate until decades later. Dad refused to make me the center of his world.

I recently stumbled upon a pretty gross disorder called Prader-Willi Syndrome (PWS). The few who are diagnosed with this annually never get full when they eat. Left without the sensation of satisfaction the individual keeps eating and eating and eating, right into obesity and possibly an early grave. When an individual is afflicted with PWS, good things (like food) can become deadly things.

Many children are being over-served in the attention department. When children take the place of Jesus as the center of the home, they're set up for failure outside the home. A sociologist has quipped that ours is the boomerang age, where children leave the home only to return and settle in for extended adolescence. How did this happen? When you were the one everyone orbited around in your home, and then when you left and discovered you're not the center of the world, of course you'd want to come back to the one place you were.

In hindsight, my father's refusal to allow me to overdose on attention gave me three gifts:

1. The gift of not being number one. My parents are deep lovers of Jesus, and they always reminded us that we've been called into something so much bigger than us, the kingdom. Our extracurricular activities were scheduled around church attendance, missions trips and service projects (not the other way around).

2. The gift of seeing a man work. Dad's absence communicated loudly, he works. When kids (on occasion) would ask where my dad was. I could tell them he was at work. Work is a good thing. His work paid for my athletic fees, cleats, equipment and uniforms.

3. Resilience. Children are a lot more resilient than we give them credit. My father was easily gone over 100 days a year, and that's a conservative estimate. While he came to everything he could, he missed a lot. What were the results? Me and my siblings live in almost every region of the country hundreds and thousands of miles away from our parents and each other, where we've had to start lives and build churches, businesses and community. We've got a grit to us because our parents refused to coddle. Thanks dad (and mom).

So relax. Missing a game or a recital isn't a bad thing, it can actually do your children some good.

The point in sharing this is not to suggest that we were perfect parents or that we have a perfect marriage. We've made our share of mistakes, and there certainly were times in which I wished I was home more and attended more ball games and recitals. But because we sought to build our marriage and family around the Lordship of Christ and His plan for us, He has blessed our marriage and family in ways that humble us and fill our hearts with great joy.

2. Feed the relationship.

To be married means to not only acknowledge that we need each other, but to look to each other as primary sources of growth and development. Once again, this is what God meant when He said in Genesis 2:18, "Then the LORD God said, 'It is not good that the man should be alone; I will make him a helper fit for him.'" As we mentioned in chapter 1, marriage was instituted to meet our aloneness needs ("not good that the man should be *alone*" [emphasis added]). Our marriage partner is a "helper fit" for us.

Yes, God is speaking of providing Adam a wife. However, it is wrong to conclude that the man is the only one who has the aloneness need and is the one who needs a "helper" (although Karen would say that I do need a lot of help!). The apostle Paul says in Ephesians 5:29 that husbands are to nourish and cherish their wives. In short, we get married to nurture and care for each other.

Anything that is alive needs to be fed. We've all seen on the news stories of owners who were charged and even arrested for neglecting their pets. Often these reports show footage of gaunt, starving animals with a paper-thin layer of skin barely covering their ribs. You're left shaking your head, wondering how somebody could be so cruel and uncaring. But I would guess that most of these pet owners didn't set out to abuse these animals. They got distracted, caught up in other things, in over their heads. They stopped taking care of the very thing they wanted.

We meet couples that are starving to death. Somewhere along the line, they made some wrong assumptions about each other and about the marriage. Like the couple who were married for fifteen years with three beautiful kids, living in an upscale community. He comes home one day to an empty house and finds a note on the kitchen counter that says, "I can't take it anymore. I feel empty, alone, and uncared for. Our marriage has been dying for years. I want out."

At first he is shocked and devastated. But over the next few weeks, he realizes that his wife had been sending him signals for the last few years. "Can we get away for the weekend?" "I'd like to spend some time with you this evening." "I need your help with the kids." "I have this idea, this dream, can you help me with it?" Most of the time he was so busy pursuing his career and his hobbies,

It's difficult to stay
angry at each
other when you
pray together.

he would either minimize what his wife was saying or put her off.

Love is more than a feeling. It is commitment. It is action. It is doing and responding to those we love by *showing* them the central place they have in our hearts. This is what we mean by "feeding" the relationship. It is making consistent, heart-nourishing deposits in each other's lives. How do we do this? Here are a few suggestions.

Regularly read the Bible as a couple. Share what God is teaching you from His Word. Make this part of the rhythm of your relationship and interaction with each other. God will calibrate the marriage around His plan and purposes for you as a couple and a family.

Pray together every day. The very act of prayer is an expression of our need for God to intervene for us. It expresses our dependence on Him and it draws us closer to His heart. It also draws us closer together as couples and deepens and sweetens our intimacy with each other. Besides, it's difficult to stay angry at each other when you pray together.

Lighten each other's load. Proactively look for ways to free the other from some of the responsibilities they're carrying—picking up around the house, disciplining the children, cleaning up after meals, or helping with a challenge they're facing at work. Think of ways in which you can come alongside of each other to help relieve pressure and burdens.

Identify what refreshes your spouse. Encourage them to spend time doing the things that put wind in their sails. Spend time with them doing what they love to do, even if it's not your cup of tea. For example, a round of golf refreshes me. Karen does not play and frankly is not crazy about the game. But she will ride with me in the cart and show genuine interest in my game. Why? Because she knows how much I enjoy playing golf.

Serve together. There is something about giving yourselves as a couple in serving the needs of others that infuses gratitude and richness in your relationship. It reminds us that our marriage is not just about us. Find ways to serve as a couple. Perhaps it's going on a missions trip, hosting a small group, or volunteering at a local ministry.

Spend regular, uninterrupted time together. I'm not talking about sitting in the same room watching TV together, but spending time listening to each other's hearts and dreaming and planning together. Take the time to really hear and savor what the other is thinking and feeling. Carve out some time each evening to touch base with each other. Schedule two or three weekends a year to get away as a couple to talk and connect on a deeper level.

Nourishing each other is intentional. It takes time, focus, and discipline. Our attitude toward our spouse should be that we don't want to withdraw more than we deposit.

This leads to the next guideline . . .

3. *Decide on and keep boundaries.*

Boundaries are necessary in order to know the outline of your property. We need to know where our property ends and where our neighbor's begins. We invite trouble when we don't acknowledge and respect the property lines. It's like the guy who looked out his kitchen window one morning and saw the neighbor planting a vegetable garden in his yard!

Boundaries are also important barriers to keep intruders out. Fences. Walls. Gates. Security systems. We use these things in order to protect what is dear, valuable, and important to us. Thriving marriages are always on the watch for home invaders. If not, then what is important and vital to the marriage will be stolen away over time.

King Solomon underscored the importance of boundaries when he said in Proverbs 5:15–17, "Drink water from your own cistern, flowing water from your own well. Should your springs be scattered abroad, streams of water in the streets? Let them be for yourself alone, and not for strangers with you." The point is we must value and protect the relationship. We should not trespass those boundaries, and neither should we allow others to trespass them. With this in mind, we made a commitment to our adult children that we would not give them unsolicited advice and we would honor and respect their marriages and families as their first priority.

But before we can establish boundaries, we need to know what needs to be protected. What is important to us and to our family? How are we going to use our time? How do we handle and respond to unsolicited advice from parents, family, and friends? How do we make decisions about commitments that affect the marriage and the family? How do we protect the goals, dreams, and aspirations we have? A thriving marriage is intentional. If we don't have fences to outline and safeguard our property, then squatters will set up shop on land that belongs to us.

4. Respect and leverage your differences.

Most married couples have significant differences in certain areas—temperament, decision making, interests, and more. Sometimes those very differences are what attracted us to each other. Sometimes we minimize those differences in our early days as a couple and think the other will change.

Whatever the case, after we've been married a while we realize those differences are inescapable. What once was cute and attractive is now quirky and irritating. The differences rub us the wrong way. The temptation is to give our spouse a makeover, transforming them into our image and likeness. The battle begins. And the outcome is not pretty. Anger. Frustration. Resentment. Isolation.

At this point we need to make a very important distinction: weaknesses and differences are not necessarily the same thing. We should help each other to grow and overcome our weaknesses and deficiencies. We want to help each other to be all that God intended for us to be. But weaknesses are addressed and changed in a climate saturated with love, grace, and acceptance.

We need to figure out a way to harness our differences and leverage them to make the relationship stronger and better than it could ever be by denying or fighting our differences. This creates synergy. *Synergy* is "the interaction of elements that when combined produce a total effect that is greater than the sum of the individual elements, contributions, etc." (dictionary. com). Let's not waste our differences. Use them.

Karen and I have a lot in common, but in many ways we are very different. For example, Karen has an eye for detail and is an excellent administrator. I'm sort of a "big picture" guy, and the energy gets drained out of me if I get pulled into managing details. Through the years we have learned how to leverage our strengths and to compensate for our weaknesses. But notice I said we *learned* how to do this.

For example, the first couple of years of our marriage I thought leading our home meant that I managed the money. I wasn't good at it and, honestly, I didn't like doing it. But I thought because I was the "head" of the house, then managing the checkbook was part of the job description. It wasn't working. The combination of being insecure and frustrated is torture. Karen was frustrated too. Can you imagine? Here I am thinking that my "manhood" is on the line, but I'm making a mess. Karen is saying, "Why don't you let me help you? I love doing this stuff!" Survival was at stake, and humility finally kicked in. One of the best things I've ever done was to turn to Karen and say, "Sweetheart, I'm doing a lousy job. I'm not good at this and I need your help." We turned a corner. Synergy.

In 1 Peter 3:7 we read, "Likewise, husbands, live with your wives in an understanding way." This implies that we know who she is, how she thinks, and what gifts, talents, and abilities she possesses. But I don't think that this is just some kind of passive understanding. I think it means that we appreciate, value, and leverage both who she is and what God has given to her to bring to the table. Again, God brings two people together so that they could be better and more than they could be without each other.

> God brings two people together so that they could be better and more than they could be without each other.

If there's one thing we've learned, it is that a thriving marriage means that couples have learned to hold two things in tension. First, the two of us are different *so that* as a couple we are far more effective than we can be on our own. View the differences as gifts and not barriers. Second, a commitment to marriage is a commitment to change. To leverage our differences does not mean that we don't encourage and help each other to grow and change.

If we're not better, different people *because* of the marriage, then something is wrong with the marriage. We will talk more about this later.

5. *Protect and defend each other without denying the truth.*

There should be no question as to whether or not our spouse is committed to us and if they have our back. We defend and protect each other because we indeed are one. Our love and devotion should never be questioned. And when it is tested, we don't flinch or hesitate. The message should be clear. If you have a problem with Crawford, then you have a problem with Karen. If you have a problem with Karen, then you have a problem with Crawford. Marriage is a package deal.

But protecting and defending each other does not mean that we turn a blind eye to the truth. During these forty-seven years of marriage, we have had our share of hard, painful conversations about things that we didn't necessarily want to hear but that we needed to hear. We have had seasons in which one or both of us were criticized and even attacked. There were those times in which we had to face the raw reality about our inadequacies and weaknesses. Truth can be painful and intimidating. It exposes what we are trying to hide, often revealing our fears and insecurities. But what's the alternative? Layers of denial. Loss of intimacy. Pretense. Isolation.

As couples we need to cultivate the ability to face and extract the truth from outside criticism as well as developing an ear to hear and receive the truth from the person who has committed their lives to us. There can be no true intimacy apart from truth. Remember, once Adam and Eve embraced lies, shame and guilt replaced freedom and transparency (Gen. 3:7).

Truth is the vehicle by which God not only captures our attention but gets us headed in the right direction. Ephesians 4:15 says, "Speaking the truth in love we are to grow up in every way into him who is the head, into Christ."

But truth is to be shared in *love*. It is precisely because we love each other that we not only want the best for each other but we also want our spouse to be all that God intended for them to be. This requires that we share the truth with consideration, grace, and kindness—but still, we have to share the truth. When Karen says to me, "Honey, you know I love you, but . . . " I need to take a deep breath and get ready to receive some insight and truth.

Marriage, like the Christian life, is not a pain-free experience. But the pain is necessary to experience health, meaningful change, and growth. And this is God's goal for every follower of Christ.

6. Identify and pursue God's plan for your marriage.

As we discussed in chapter 1, God has an overarching plan and purpose for marriage. But more specifically, God has a plan for *your* marriage. God has a unique mark and expression of His character and glory He wants to make through us as couples during our moment in history. The anchor question we have to keep coming back to is, "What does God want to do through our marriage and through our family?" Far too many of us are simply satisfied with making what we call "family environment" issues the barometer of the quality of the marriage. You know: Are we getting along? Are we managing and resolving our conflicts? Are we keeping our heads above water financially? Are we spending quality time with each other?

To be sure, these are important considerations. However, the positive answers to these questions still don't provide the soul-satisfying fulfillment that comes from embracing and aligning our marriage to God's will and plan for us as a couple.

Romans 12:1-2 says, "I appeal to you therefore, brothers, by the mercies of God, to present your bodies as a living sacrifice, holy and acceptable to God, which is your spiritual worship. Do not be conformed to this world, but be transformed by the renewal of your mind, that by testing you may discern what is the will of God, what is good and acceptable and perfect." Notice, there is this appeal to place all that we are ("bodies") as a living sacrifice in God's hands; a command not to be shaped and molded into the way in which this world thinks and what it values; a charge to renew our minds so that we see all of life through God's eyes. All of this so that we "may discern what is the will of God." True for us as individuals; true in marriage.

> Our heart's desire should be that we do not want to miss anything that God wants to do through us as a couple.

Let's not make assumptions about God's plan for our marriage. Make a habit of grabbing your spouse's hand and dropping to your knees before an open Bible, asking God to show you what He wants. Then ask Him for the courage to do what He shows you.

Remember, a river without banks is a swamp. These six guidelines will help us keep the "river" flowing in the right direction. But if these are the guidelines, then what are some of the habits that will enrich the journey? That's what the next chapter is about.

To think about . . .

How do you respond to the reflections of Crawford and Karen's son Bryan on his dad sometimes not being there?

What might it look like for you and your spouse to become a "kingdom couple" or build a "kingdom family"? What gets in the way?

4

The Habits That Transform a Marriage

Crawford: *Every night before my mother went to bed she would get on her knees and pray—out loud—for her family and other needs on her heart. It is difficult to put in words the impact this has had on me. Growing up, there were a number of times I was on the verge of making some wrong choices, and the picture of Mom on her knees crying out to God for me would stop me in my tracks. Her humble, quiet strength came from this consistent habit of turning to God for His intervention and wisdom. Seeing mom consistently and unashamedly pray served as a powerful motivation for me and my two sisters to cultivate this life-transforming habit.*

It's sort of funny. Mom never said a lot about praying, she just did it consistently. In much the same way, when our kids were growing up, we had family devotions. I don't recall telling our children to do the same with their families. But it's interesting that they do. The lesson: consistently model the right stuff.

Karen and I can annoy each other. We've been married for so long we know what buttons to push—and what buttons never to push. But sometimes we annoy each other just because of some stubborn habit. A few of these habits are so ingrained in us that we have learned to not only live with them but in a weird way they have become endearing. It's sort of part of what makes Karen "Karen" and Crawford "Crawford."

Habits. We all have them. Some good, some bad, some just irritating. Dr. Gary Chapman, author of *The 5 Love Languages*, has written about how his wife, Karolyn, does not close drawers. A small thing, but annoying to her husband in the early years of their marriage! But in time he learned it was just easier to close the drawer rather than have a silly argument.

We all have habits that are "second nature"—showering, taking the same route to work every day. We all have habits we need to get rid of. And we all need to cultivate good habits.[1] So the challenge is identifying the good habits and then disciplining ourselves to consistently practice them so that over time they become an essential, natural part of our lives and behavior.

But some habits cannot be broken simply by the force of our will. These habits are anchored in the stubborn, debilitating nature of sin. Try as we might, no amount of effort on our part is going to release their grip on us. Even the strong, resilient apostle Paul had to confess, "For I do not understand my own actions. For I do not do what I want, but I do the very thing I hate" (Rom. 7:15). The context of this confession is Paul's testimony concerning his ongoing struggle with sin. He couldn't get rid of that which was ingrained in him—sin and disobedience. It affected his behavior. It's the same with us.

Some habits cannot be broken simply by the force of our will.

1. Braco Pobric, "What Are Habits?," The Positive Psychology People, http://www.thepositive psychologypeople.com/habits-to-happiness/.

Three Life-Giving Habits

Karen and I want to identify and underscore three enduring habits that each couple together must press into and make "second nature" in order for our marriages to reflect God's purpose and mission for this and future generations. The habits we want to highlight are those that are anchored in our character and our relationship with the Lord. That's not to say that stuff like consistently picking up after yourself, paying your bills on time, or keeping your mouth closed when you eat are not good habits to practice. But we want to focus on those habits that give enduring life to the marriage.

These foundational habits are not developed solely by the force of our will. We are sinners. We have sinned and we have been sinned against. Thus, some of our habits, actions, and responses have been shaped and informed by sin. So much so that, as Paul says, we do not understand our own actions. The solution to our sin is the gospel, the good news of Jesus' death, burial, and resurrection (1 Cor. 15:3-4). Christ's death on the cross not only paid the penalty for our sin but has broken the power of sin's control over us (Eph. 2:1-10). What's more, the moment we turn to Christ and place our faith in Him, we receive forgiveness, and the Holy Spirit comes to permanently take up residence in our lives (Eph. 1:13-14).

This is the reason why the apostle Paul's story doesn't end with the confession of his struggle with sin (Rom. 7:15). But in Romans chapter 8, he celebrates his forgiveness through the work of Christ and that, yes, indeed, he can overcome his sinful habits through the presence and power of the Holy Spirit (Rom. 8:1-17).

We have had the joy and privilege of being exposed to many

"until-death-do-us-part" marriages. These are couples that have been married for fifty years or more. What we have witnessed and learned from them is that thriving, successful marriages are built on humility and dependence. These couples were aware of their inadequacies and imperfections. They needed God's help. They learned to bring their sinful habit patterns to the Lord and asked Him to show them the foundational habit patterns that breathe supernatural, transformative life into their marriage and then to give them the power, through His Spirit, to develop and exercise these habits.

Caution: developing and nurturing these habits takes commitment and work. The story of hope and growth is not simply the product of clear thinking or some "secret" insight that brought us to a glorious tipping point. But because we love each other and we want our relationship to tell the truth about God, and our marriage to reflect His plan and purposes, we step toward the challenge and embrace the pain.

So what are the baseline, repetitive, consistent, transformative behaviors (habits) exhibited by couples that are committed to developing a godly marriage that will affect and impact their moment in history as well as future generations?

First, we consistently pursue Christlikeness individually and as a couple.

This is both a goal and a habit. The first thing every morning, Karen can be found sitting at the kitchen table with her open Bible and her prayer journal. This is not just some ritual that she goes through. She is nurturing and feeding her soul. She is listening to the Lord as He speaks to her heart through His Word, listening to the guidance of the Holy Spirit. She is talking to the Lord in prayer about the challenges she is facing, the needs of our family, the cares and concerns of others. And I know she is praying for me. She is deepening her relationship with the Lord. This habit, this commitment, has marked her life. It has created in her a delightful longing to live in God's presence and to center her life and all that concerns her around the one she loves the most, Jesus.

I, too, have a similar routine. Many years ago, I made a commitment to the Lord that before I spoke to anyone else, I would speak to Him in prayer. Every morning I spend time reading His Word and, most mornings, capturing in my prayer journal what I sense the Lord is saying to me. I pray for those who are hurting, have needs, and are facing challenges. And I pray for Karen. How I treasure these daily appointments with the Lord. The more time we spend with Him, the more we want to be with Him and to be like Him. Jesus becomes the joy and passion of our lives.

Our children have all commented that seeing us nurture and pursue this habit has had a profound impact on them. No, Karen and I didn't do this *primarily* to make an impression on our children. We walked toward our relationship with the Lord because we are convinced that apart from Him we can do nothing. In so doing, we have tasted the incredible joy and power that comes when we bask in His presence. We have experienced Him stepping into the challenges we have faced in our marriage and raising our children. This active dependence on Him has been "caught" by our children. It brings tender, joy-filled tears to our eyes as we witness our children building their marriages and families around the pursuit of Christlikeness. Jesus is the life and message of marriage and family.

As Karen and I have grown in our walk and relationship with Christ, He has placed in our hearts a "holy impatience" (or at least we hope it is!) with complacency or an incremental approach to our journey toward Christlikeness. I suppose some of this has to do with where we are at this stage in our lives. You could say we have more road behind us than we do in front of us. But life is uncertain. And ultimately the only thing—the only One—worth pursuing and giving ourselves to is Jesus.

But what does looking like Jesus, well, look like? Galatians 5:22–23 lists the fruit of the Spirit. These nine characteristics are also a composite portrait of Christlikeness: "But the fruit of the Spirit is love, joy, peace, patience, kindness, goodness, faithfulness, gentleness, self-control; against such things there is no law." Once again, as we develop this glorious habit of pursuing Christlikeness, these nine characteristics (and more) become an ever-increasing reality.

When He is first, His work in our lives becomes evident. He changes us and removes the sinful irritants in our lives. It's not so much that we grow into a better version of ourselves; we start looking more and more like Jesus. Karen and I often comment that as we have gotten older, we look more like our parents. In fact, the other day I picked up a picture of my father and could not believe how much I look like him. But this analogy breaks down. Looking like our parents is genetic. Looking like Jesus is intentional.

Perhaps you're in a marriage where, frankly, pursuing Christlikeness is not at the top of the list. Other things or relationships are more important. Your affections have been captured by someone or something else. You are Christians and good people. By most measurements, you have a good marriage. But consistently pursuing Christ has, honestly, become more of an erratic hobby than a habit. And if you were completely honest, you don't really see this as something you ought to throw yourself into right now. You conclude that you'll get there one day, but for now "God knows and understands where we are."

Keep in mind, however, that the more we put off changing, the more difficult it is to change. In fact, we become resistant to the very thing we know that we need. We grow accustomed to self-reliance and we have become at home with accommodating less than what we know God has for us and wants us to be and pursue.

And besides, consider what your children and those close to you are missing. What lasting, eternal weight are you modeling before them and placing in their hands? Who and what is going to give them hope, stability, and lasting joy and satisfaction? No, we need to do a lot more than just tell them what matters most. They need to see, taste, and feel the delightful effects of the habitual, focused pursuit of Christlikeness through those God has assigned to give shape to their lives and commission their future.

> We can become resistant to the very thing we know that we need.

Second, we consistently *focus on character and integrity.*

Character and integrity are the building blocks of trust and confidence. But—they don't come naturally to us.

Back to the beginning. After God brings Eve to Adam and establishes the vision and nature of marriage (Gen. 2:24), we read this wonderful, compelling description of the first couple's innocence and transparency: "And the man and his wife were both naked and were not ashamed" (v. 25). They weren't guilty or embarrassed because, frankly, they had nothing to hide. They were both a clear, clean picture window that each could look out of and peer into without obstruction. When they looked at each other they saw everything there was to see.

But this didn't last long. Satan deceived them. They disobeyed God, and sin entered their reality and into the world. Guilt, shame, and hiding has been our default mode ever since.

Yes, when we trust Christ as Savior and Lord He forgives us of our sin and makes us His child. But He doesn't remove our ability to sin or the inclination to sin. We have to cultivate an appetite for obedience, for consistently doing the right, godly thing. Again, character and integrity are not givens. They must be developed.

And in marriage, we bring who we are, and who we are not, to the relationship. We should never stop working on developing wholeness and transparency in the marriage. More than anything else, we want it to be said that we are worthy of each other's trust.

Some years ago, Karen and I were speaking at a marriage conference. During a break, a man approached me and said that his wife doesn't trust him. He told me that he had been involved in a long-term affair that he had relatively recently ended. He had repented of his adultery, and he and his wife were working on repairing the damage to their marriage. But he was frustrated. He couldn't seem to understand how his wife could say that she forgave him but didn't trust him.

I pointed out what I suspect he already knew. Forgiveness and trust are not the same thing. I told him that she shouldn't give him the gift of trust just yet. He had broken his marriage vows and for months lied to her and betrayed her trust and confidence. Now he had to intentionally demonstrate over time that he was willing to do whatever it took to recapture her heart and confidence.

More than anything, we want it to be said that we are worthy of each other's trust.

Character and integrity represent the fiber and fabric of a marriage. There is nothing to build the marriage on, let alone to place in the hands of the next generation, if there is the collapse of character. But it is fragile. If we're not vigilant, sin and neglect will ambush us and wash away the trust and confidence that's taken years, a lifetime, to build. We have to be consciously aware that we are stewards of this trust and confidence. It is a treasured gift. Thus, we are working on this trust, preserving it, not taking it for granted. It is a *habit.*

Character and integrity are interrelated. Integrity means to be whole or undivided. It is the idea of not just affirming clear guiding principles and values, but living in light of them. Further, it is behavior that is consistent with the promises and commitments that we make. We do what we say we are and what we value. If we make a promise, we keep it.

Psalm 15 paints an inviting picture of what integrity looks like:

O LORD, who shall sojourn in your tent?
Who shall dwell on your holy hill?

He who walks blamelessly and does what is right
and speaks truth in his heart;
who does not slander with his tongue
and does no evil to his neighbor,
nor takes up a reproach against his friend;
in whose eyes a vile person is despised,

but who honors those who fear the LORD;
who swears to his own hurt and does not change;
who does not put out his money at interest
    and does not take a bribe against the innocent.
He who does these things shall never be moved.

Now to be sure, no one this side of heaven is a perfect picture of integrity. We are all flawed, fallen human beings. But neither should this reality serve as an excuse or justification for erratic, inconsistent behavior and a failure to keep our commitments and promises. We must press into closing the gap between what we say and how we behave. After all, the gift of trust is an expression of confidence, and confidence is earned through observed consistency.

My parents believed this. Honesty and integrity were core values to Crawford and Sylvia Loritts. What a great blessing and gift this was to my sisters and me! (In fact, I wrote a book in tribute to my dad. The title of the book is *Never Walk Away: Lessons on Integrity from a Father Who Lived It.*) This sounds remarkable . . . but it's true. Our parents never made a promise or commitment to us that they did not keep. There were occasions that something beyond their control came up and they had to fulfill the commitment later. But they didn't just forget about it. They did what they said they would do.

This created an environment of trust and stability. What's more, my parents trusted each other, and as kids we saw this and felt it. This gave us the gift of security. I remember glancing at my father during our wedding ceremony and thinking, "By God's grace I'm going to fulfill my vows and commitment to Karen the way you did for Mom."

For twenty-seven years Karen and I served on the staff of Cru, a large, worldwide ministry committed to sharing the hope of the gospel with every person in the world. During those early years I traveled a lot, speaking on college campuses across the country. I was away from Karen and the kids sometimes for several weeks at a time. When I checked into a hotel or motel, the first thing I did was to take a picture out of my briefcase and put it on the mirror. That picture would be the last thing I looked at when I left the room and the first thing I looked at when I returned. The message was, "Crawford, you're one decision away from stupid. These are the most important people in the world—don't do anything to hurt them or to violate the gift of their trust and confidence." I was reminded that I had to keep my promise to them.

> I heard a friend say, "When we are born, we look like our parents. When we die, we look like our decisions."

So you can imagine how deeply moved Karen and I were as we listened to our oldest son, Bryan, a few years ago when he said to an audience that "my parents never made a promise to me or my siblings that they did not keep." No, we were not and are not perfect, but Karen and I have taken seriously the commitment to develop the *habit* of integrity.

Character is the composite picture of our choices, decisions, and how we have responded to life and its challenges. It's kind of like when we say that an older house has a lot of "character." I think what we mean is that the house sort of tells the story of the life that has been lived inside its walls. We, too, tell the story of the choices and decisions we have made. I heard a friend say, "When we are born, we look like our parents. When we die, we look like our decisions."

Again, integrity and character are related. Fundamentally, if we are dishonest and ignore or disregard our commitments and responsibilities, we will have poor or weak character. Dishonesty and irresponsibility become embedded in who and what we have become. Over time we will look like what we have or have not done and not necessarily what we have said. This indeed is the real stuff of credibility and legacy.

Marriage models not only what God wants to do in every generation but also places on display what our children and the next generation should become. In this regard, marriage is incarnational. Our character has to match what we say we believe and value. We keep a close watch over our decisions and behavior to make sure they are telling the truth about where we are headed and in line with the noble vision of what God has called us to be. It is our heart's desire that our lives are far more eloquent than our words. There is simply too much at stake.

Strong, compelling marriages are the product of strong, compelling character. It is not just that these couples have mastered the "how-tos" of a good relationship. They pay attention to what's underneath the hood. They've made the conscious commitment that, by God's grace, they will not let anything in their character be a stumbling block to each other and their children. They are committed to making things right.

Third, we consistently face the reality of our humanity with a willingness to forgive.

But what do we do when we mess up, when we have made poor choices and even betrayed the confidence and trust of our marriage partner? There is grace and mercy with our great God.

Karen and I know couples that have made painful, heartbreaking choices. Some have committed adultery. In another case, the marriage was shaken because it was discovered that the husband was embezzling funds from his job. And so on, all the poor choices and bad decisions we fallen humans make. But thankfully, in many of these cases God brought repentance and reconciliation. When these spouses turned to the Lord, not only did they find forgiveness, but they also received God's enabling power to repair and rebuild their character.

Failure doesn't have to be a life sentence. Consider David, who committed murder and adultery (2 Sam. 11). When he repented, God put him back together and wonderfully restored him (2 Sam. 12:1–14; Ps. 51). And God will do the same for all of us if we turn to Him. He will put us back on track. However, there are sometimes unintended consequences when we sin, and the road back may be steeper than we anticipated.

Most couples when they get married underestimate their sinfulness. I know this was our case. You may have heard the old line, "Love is blind but marriage is an eye-opener." There's more truth to that than we might care to admit. I didn't realize the depths of my selfishness until Karen and I got married. And it wasn't just me. Karen began to see more clearly some of her own "stuff" that she needed to deal with as well.

Contrary to our romantic vision and idealism, we don't marry a deity or an angel. Neither do we marry a vision of what that person can be or what we think we can make them—that's a losing proposition. We marry who that person *is*.

Does that mean we never change? No. Karen and I, in many ways, are completely different people than we were when we got

married. God has used our marriage and our love and commitment to each other to encourage us to grow and to change. By
definition growth means change. Further, a commitment to be
married means a commitment to change. If there is no growth
toward the Lord and toward each other, there is no true intimacy—
and that means change.

Here's what I mean when I say that we "marry who that person is." It means that only fallen people get married. We carry in
us the stain of sin. And the closer we get to each other, the more
we see the sin, failures, and shortcomings.

> **A commitment to be married means a commitment to change.**

When I was in high school, I had the
privilege of singing in a choir at the iconic
Carnegie Hall in New York City. The lights
were turned up during the rehearsal and
I was a bit surprised at how "imperfect"
and unimpressive the stage area was. But from the audience,
with just the right lighting, it was inviting, even spectacular.
When we get married, the lights are turned up. We discover
things that we hadn't fully recognized before. Frankly, some
of these things are offensive and irritating. We are confronted
with the stain of sin.

So what do we do? Go down the path of trying to fix the other
person? That tends not to end well. Depending on the personality
and disposition, we encounter either direct, obvious resistance or
passive-aggressive behavior. As we have pointed out, there's stuff
in us that we can't get rid of on our own. That's the nature of sin.
In fact, we can sincerely pour ourselves into doing better and trying harder but still not get anywhere. Further, change is frustrated
when we come across to our spouse as if we are the model and

standard in the area with which they are struggling. Remember, *both* of us are sinners and have stuff that we struggle to overcome. We need a Savior. Karen is not Crawford's Savior. Crawford is not Karen's Savior. Jesus is our Savior. We have been forgiven and we need forgiveness. We need to lovingly come alongside each other and encourage our marriage partner to tap into our life-giving, loving Savior for His grace and help to be what only He can make us.

The way we do this is through humility, and by practicing the habit of giving and receiving forgiveness. The Bible says in Ephesians 4:32, "Be kind to one another, tenderhearted, forgiving one another, as God in Christ forgave you." This verse drips with grace. Notice the sweet, compelling words: "kind," "tenderhearted," "forgiving." This indeed should form our attitude and demeanor toward each other as couples and underlie the atmosphere we create in the relationship and in the home.

It is within this relational context that we address irritating habits and offenses. What's more, although the word *humility* is not used in this verse, the *attitude* of humility is clear. We are to forgive "as God in Christ forgave you." Because we are mindful that God has forgiven us through the unimaginable sacrifice of His Son, we can and must graciously forgive others.

When God forgives us, what does He do? *He releases the offense and chooses not to relate to us based on the offense.* When we forgive, we too are choosing to release the offense and not allow the offense to be a barrier in the relationship. One of the ways that we know that we have forgiven someone is that we don't remind them of what they did to hurt or offend us. If we can't resist the urge to bring the matter up, then it is a pretty clear indication that we have not forgiven the person. We've not let it go. Certainly, forgiveness is not always easy. But if we choose not to forgive, we are building a wall that will serve as a permanent barrier to intimacy and we are solidifying anger, bitterness, and resentment.

Forgiveness is the gift of grace. We offend God and hurt His heart, but rather than assigning us to permanent punishment, He reaches out to us, and through His amazing love, He pours out His kindness over us. We can do the same as we extend—or accept—the gift, and experience this sweet, uncontaminated, unconditional love.

Karen and I stopped pretending that we are more than we really are and less needy than the other person.

We don't perform for it. We can't bargain for it. It doesn't come with a price tag. It is a gift. I can't put into words the tenderness and sweetness that washes over me when I know I've done something to offend Karen and she turns to me and says, "Sweetheart, I forgive you." Karen feels the same when I express my forgiveness for something that she has done.

The habit of giving and receiving forgiveness is liberating. A grace-filled home creates an inviting atmosphere for wholesome, authentic change. It has a way of flushing out hypocrisy and protecting us from the heart erosion that comes from pride-based performance. In the name of being a good example, sometimes I think we unintentionally step into hypocrisy. We deny or minimize our weaknesses and failures. The problem is everyone in the house knows that we're not everything that we are projecting to be. Wouldn't it be much better to acknowledge our imperfections and need for help and forgiveness? Again, Karen and I are more motivated to change because we stopped pretending that we are more than we really are and somehow less needy than the other person.

Finally, this models to our children and grandchildren that we are always forgiven sinners, and it is God's amazing grace that gets us to where we need to be.

So to sum up, the consistent pursuit of Christlikeness, the consistent cultivation of character and integrity, and giving and receiving the gift of forgiveness are foundational habits that bring richness, trust, and intimacy to the marriage. Now let's look at some other gifts our spouse needs from us.

To think about . . .

Crawford shares how he and Karen "stopped pretending that we are more than we really are and somehow less needy than the other person." Have you seen this "pretending" in your marriage? How have you dealt (or not dealt) with it?

5

Gifts: What Every Wife Needs

Crawford: *Work was very important to Pop. He took his responsibility to provide for his family seriously. For more than thirty years, he worked in a warehouse for the A&P grocery chain, unloading and loading trucks. In addition, he sometimes picked up extra work so that we could enjoy vacations and other things we wanted. He bought my sisters and me our first cars. If we had a need, he figured out a way to meet it. He made sure that, to the best of his ability, his wife and family were cared for.*

We never heard him complain about having to go to work or that the responsibility for caring for us was an unwelcome burden and chore. In fact, after he retired, he loved to tell his grandkids about the joy and privilege of being able to work and take care of their Nanna and parents. Sure, he'd made many sacrifices along the way. But he viewed sacrifice as the privilege and opportunity to invest in what mattered most.

What a gift!

Not in the sense of bringing home some expensive jewelry for your wife or a new TV for your kids. No, this is much deeper and more enduring. One of the tests of true love is the answer to the question, "How much am I willing to sacrifice for this person?"

When we're in love, we *want* to give. When we are married, we daily *get* the opportunity to focus on our marriage partner and make the kind of deposits in them that will bring joy, strength, and sweetness to the relationship. In fact, *the depth and richness of our marriage is a reflection of the sacrificial deposits we have made both for the marriage and in each other's lives over time.* Since marriage is the sacred conduit by which the image of God is to be passed from one generation to the next and intended to be an inviting portrait of Christlikeness to a watching world, what gifts should we be giving to each other?

In this chapter and the next, Karen and I want to answer that question. First, we will take a look at the gifts that every wife needs from her husband. Then in the next chapter we will look at the gifts that every husband needs from his wife.

The first gift that a husband and wife should give to each other is *godliness*. We've talked at length about this in the previous chapter. But it is hard to say too much about how our relationship with the Lord shapes, sustains, and transforms a marriage. In fact, the greatest contribution we make to *every* relationship in life is our intentional pursuit of godliness. Being and becoming what we need to be for each other in marriage takes more than reading a few books and attending a couple of marriage conferences and seminars. The real hope and blessing to the marriage is the work of God in our hearts.

But what, specifically, does every wife need from her husband? Here's Karen's list.

"Husbands, Love Your Wives"

First, the gift of *unconditional love*. Ephesians 5:25–28 says, "Husbands, love your wives, as Christ loved the church and gave himself up for her. . . . He who loves his wife loves himself."

On our wedding day, Karen and I committed to love and cherish each other in sickness and in health, for better for worse, for richer for poorer, until death us do part. But she felt insecure, inadequate, and fearful. She was aware of her brokenness and the lingering effects of the pain and dysfunction in her home. She struggled with resentment and bitterness. Years later she shared with me that on the last evening of our honeymoon she stared into the bathroom mirror with tears streaming down her cheeks because she was afraid that she would fall victim to the cycle of broken marriages and relationships that was all too common in her family.

During those early months of our marriage, the fear and insecurity at times caused her to be a bit distant and not always responsive to my affection. I was confused, and believe me, I didn't always respond the right or the best way.

Karen says it was my love for her and constant pursuit of her that God used to build hope and confidence. Trust me, I didn't do this perfectly. But we had promised to commit ourselves to an enduring love for each other. Vows and promises become cherished commitments when they are tested and threatened, and we choose to live by them.

> Karen loved my parents and was drawn to their example, to the sweetness of their relationship.

We're all touched by the young couple with the promise of a bright future standing there at the altar, peering into each other's eyes and promising what they *intend* to do and be for each other.

But we are filled with hope, encouragement, and inspiration when we see couples that have been married for fifty years and hear their story of choosing to love during sometimes-dark, challenging times. They don't question the reality of their love for each other. They know it. They've experienced it. They have the war stories declaring love's victory.

Karen loved my parents and was drawn to their example and the sweetness of their relationship. She saw a couple who genuinely loved and cared for each other. She was especially drawn to how Pop treated Mom. This made a huge impression on her. She saw that although Pop was not given to "public displays of affection," he showed his love for Mom through acts of service. For example, every week Pop did the grocery shopping and loved to serve Mom in this way. (Thankfully, Karen realized early on that the "shopping gene" had not been passed on to her husband.)

She watched how he honored Mom, and how through the years they developed this uncanny ability to speak without words. It was as if they knew how to interpret each other's looks, grunts, and expressions. They seemed to know what the other needed. Pop's love for Mom was unconditional and he loved to please her, protect her, and provide for her. He was not easily driven to tears. But during their later years, Mom was hospitalized, and he was heartbroken, and the tears would trickle down his cheeks because he wanted his precious Sylvia to be all right.

Pop suffered from congestive heart failure that eventually took his life. A few weeks before he died, he said to me, "Son, take care of your mother." Sylvia was the love of his life.

Growing up with a father who modeled this kind of unconditional love and commitment marked me deeply. *Seeing* how a man should love his wife and live by his vows and promises does more for you than a thousand speeches. I am humbled when Karen says that the capacity to love in this way is in my DNA.

When our second child died shortly after birth, we were devastated, overwhelmed with grief. We were living in the Philadelphia area at the time, preparing to move to Dallas, Texas. A week before the due date, I took a quick trip to Dallas to finalize the details for the move. Then came that phone call. Sobbing, Karen said, "Crawford, the Lord has taken our baby." I was shocked. Numb. Heartbroken. I hurried to the airport and caught the first flight back to Philadelphia. All I could think about was Karen and how she was doing. I kept praying, "O God, please help us and comfort and strengthen Karen."

This was a tough time for both of us, especially Karen. There were many tears during the following weeks and months. She struggled with hurt and anger. Although I didn't know how to "fix" this, I knew that I had to turn to the Lord and be there for her and shower her with love. I drew from the example and encouragement of my father; and, besides, I had promised to love and cherish her.

This was exam time. Karen says that my response to her drew her from the brink of bitterness and depression. God in His grace and power met us at our point of need. He gave me what I needed in order to demonstrate my love for Karen, the love of my life.

When Karen speaks at marriage conferences, she will often encourage husbands to view 1 Corinthians 13:4–8 as the blueprint for expressing unconditional love to and for their wives. This kind of love is increasingly uncommon and should be our aspiration. Look at these words. "Love is patient and kind; love does not envy or boast; it is not arrogant or rude. It does not insist on its own way; it is not irritable or resentful; it does not rejoice at wrongdoing, but rejoices with the truth. Love bears all things, believes all things, hopes all things, endures all things. Love never ends." She further encourages husbands to put their name in the place of love. In other words, we should increasingly *become* what love is.

"Live with Your Wives in an Understanding Way"

Second, the gift of *understanding*. First Peter 3:7 says, "Likewise, husbands, live with your wives in an understanding way, showing honor to the woman as the weaker vessel, since they are heirs with you of the grace of life, so that your prayers may not be hindered."

Neither Karen nor I were fully prepared for what happened when we dropped our youngest daughter and last child off at college. We were now officially empty nesters. As we pulled away from the campus I felt a sadness come over me because our last child was stepping into independence. But it wasn't long before my sadness gave way to excitement. We were on the doorstep of a newfound freedom. Karen and I could do more and travel together. I was looking forward to this season, and I assumed Karen was at the same place.

Not so fast. Karen felt a deeper sense of loss than I did. In fact, in her words, she went through a bit of an emotional meltdown. For months she was visited by sadness and tears. She was surprised and discouraged by her response. She thought she was losing her "motherhood badge." Who was she now? She felt lost, lonely, alone, and insecure. I told her she had me—but that really didn't seem to help much.

Added to this, Karen was going through menopause. Neither

of us were completely prepared for the challenges the hormonal changes and our empty-nest status would present to her and our relationship. There were times she didn't want to talk about her fears or what she was feeling. In fact, she later told me that she couldn't articulate to me what was churning inside of her. Karen just wanted me to be patient and understanding, and give her a chance to resolve the emotional turmoil she was facing. And the truth is that patience is not a particular strength of mine. So often I felt bewildered and confused.

But this season, although painful, was a gift. As we walked through this, God brought us closer together and gave me greater insight into what it means to understand my wife.

Karen suggests that if you want to give your wife the gift of understanding, focus on these four Ts. The first is *time*. Be patient and approach the relationship as if you were dating again. Take the time and make the time to know what she is going through and how she is feeling. Carve out the time to get away to hang out together. She needs to know and feel that she is not just another priority in your life, she *is* your priority. Also, take the time to read Gary Chapman's excellent book *The 5 Love Languages*. Discover what her love language is, and take the time to speak it.

The second is *tenderness*. Karen let me know during that challenging time she did not want me to try to "fix" her. She wanted empathy, wrapped in tenderness. She knew that I didn't fully "get" what she was going through, but she wanted my love, encouraging words, and warm embraces. Gentleness and understanding. Acceptance and grace and not judgment. Pray for your wife, but also pray with her. Let the Lord love your wife through your responses to her.

The third is *thoughtfulness*. Do the things for her that you know she likes and enjoys. Take the initiative to make her feel special. Help to lighten her load without being asked. Watch the kids while she takes some time for herself. Avoid acting like a hotel guest in your own home. Even if your wife doesn't work outside of the home, cooking, cleaning, and laundry are constants. Pitch in and help.

The fourth is *talk*. Our wives want us to take the time to share with them not only what we're thinking but also what we're feeling. They want to hear our hearts and not just our opinions and facts. For a lot of men this is challenging. But the sweetness of transparency and oneness is experienced on a deeper level as we learn to share and trust our feelings with each other.

In addition, some of us husbands need to work on being good listeners. When Karen is sharing with me about a challenge or an issue she is facing, my first instinct is to try to come up with some ideas or options to solve the problem or address the issue. More often than not, this is not what she is looking for. She is not looking for me to say let's solve it and move on. She wants me to listen. Listening communicates value and a desire to understand.

"If Anyone Does Not Provide"

Third is the gift of *provision*. First Timothy 5:8 says, "But if anyone does not provide for his relatives, and especially for members of his household, he has denied the faith and is worse than an unbeliever."

Robert Lewis, the founder of the men's fraternity movement and the producer of the video series "33," says that manhood means "to reject passivity, accept responsibility and to lead courageously."

Men show up and do all that they can to make sure that their primary responsibility—their family—is taken care of. The Bible teaches us that to neglect to give ourselves to fulfilling this assignment is grievous to God and an affront to the very nature of our faith (1 Tim. 5:8).

No, we're not suggesting that a certain lifestyle needs to be maintained or that there are not difficult times that we will all face. Most of us have gone through those "lean" times. There are times in which it may be hard to find work. Perhaps there are health challenges. Maybe you live in an area where employment opportunities have dried up. But the point is that husbands and fathers pour themselves into making sure that their family is taken care of. They put in the time and effort to find work. Even if it is not your first, second, or third choice, your wife and family need to see you do whatever it takes to keep a roof over their heads and food on the table. Run from laziness. Work is honorable, and we were born to produce and provide.

Ultimately, God is our provider. We do all that we can to provide for our families. But we do this in such a way that it not only reflects our obedience to the word of God (1 Tim. 5:8; 2 Thess. 3:10), but it also demonstrates our dependence on God. God is our source. Sometimes the Lord will allow us to experience our need in order to prove His sufficiency.

For example, when we got married I had a year to go before I finished college. We made a decision that Karen would return to the workforce full time. She found a job working for an insurance company in Philadelphia. Finances were tight, but we were making it. Then one day Karen came home to our little apartment in tears. The city of Philadelphia had enacted a wage tax on those who did not live in the city. We lived across the bridge in Camden, NJ. Her check was $200 short. We had 50 cents to last us two weeks. We were in trouble. What were we going to do?

Karen and I dropped to our knees in our tiny living room and we cried out to God to meet our needs. We claimed His promises from His Word. At the same time, I was thinking perhaps besides the honorariums I was getting from weekend speaking engagements, I needed to get another job. I was willing to do whatever I had to in order to provide for my young bride. A few days later I was on campus and picked up some mail. I opened a letter from a man who said that he felt as if the Lord wanted him to send me a gift. Enclosed was a check for $250! I couldn't wait to share this with Karen. That evening we bowed in praise and worship to our great God for His provision.

Of course, it doesn't always happen like this. But our wives need to know that we are trusting God and willing to do whatever it takes to care and provide for them and our families.

"Love Their Wives As Their Own Bodies"

The fourth is the gift of *protection*. Ephesians 5:28 says "husbands should love their wives as their own bodies."

Karen is a very independent and competent person. She is my wife and not my daughter—my life partner, filling in the gaps in my life. She has her own thoughts, ideas, and opinions. She is capable of speaking for herself. But she wants and needs my protection. In fact, every wife needs the gift of protection from her husband.

Karen points out that there are real enemies and bullies that want to sabotage your wife. We owe it to them to protect them from any form of harm, undue stress, and danger. She needs to know that not only are you committed to her and support her, but you will do everything within your power to protect her. There should never be any doubt in her mind as to whether you will do whatever it takes to make sure she is safe.

This may mean to protect her from actual physical danger. Our kids grew up in a quiet suburban Atlanta neighborhood. Our street served as the playground for all of the kids in the neighborhood. We loved our neighbors. But there was a house that stood empty directly across from our driveway. Finally, it sold. But the house became a revolving door for a variety of shady characters who would come and go at all hours of the day and night. Never speaking to us, they would speed away with

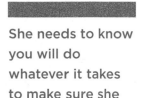

She needs to know you will do whatever it takes to make sure she is safe.

quick looks in our direction. We all were growing a bit suspicious and uneasy, especially Karen.

Then the man of the house crossed the line. Karen returned from grocery shopping and was unloading the bags out of the car when, unprovoked, he came charging toward her. He was half-dressed, sweaty, delirious, and spitting curse words at her. She left the bags and ran into the house. She told me what happened, and I went outside and had a "conversation" with our neighbor. No need to elaborate. Let's just say he gathered his senses and retreated back into his house.

We also need to protect them from emotional intruders and manipulators. Sometimes these are people who are close to us, even in our extended family. As we said earlier, boundaries are important and they have to be enforced. As husbands, the message must be clear: "You will respect my wife." This also applies to our children. Our kids need to know that raising their voice at their mother, talking back to her, or disrespecting her in any way will not be tolerated.

"Faithful in Much"

The fifth is the gift of *trust*. Luke 16:10 says, "One who is faithful in a very little is also faithful in much, and one who is dishonest in a very little is also dishonest in much."

We've talked already about the importance of character and integrity. But here we want to highlight the importance of being trustworthy. Karen says that the gift of trust comforts your wife's heart and brings peace to her mind. It builds a solid foundation for all other character traits to stand. She points out that just as being respected is a priority to a man, trust is a priceless treasure to a wife. To Karen, trust is the super glue that holds the marriage together. When trust is violated, the road back is hard and challenging.

Trust can be subtly eroded over time. When we overpromise. Don't follow through on a commitment. Weren't where we said we would be. Embellish and exaggerate the truth. Honesty becomes fluid and flexible. This kind of behavior communicates to our wives that we cannot be trusted. So she feels that she has to lower her expectations in order to protect herself from the pain of disappointment.

We all come up short and fail. But do we own up to our failures and live transparent lives? That's the question. If we want to be trusted, then we need to give our wives the gift of consistency and open, honest lives.

Sometimes the ability to be trustworthy has been sabotaged by a hidden life. There is this secret, private struggle that's been going on under the surface for quite a while, maybe years. The husband has become a master at evasion, deception, and hiding. His wife has no idea of what's going on. To further com- plicate things, the combination of shame

> We all come up short and fail. But do we own up to our failures?

and pride keeps him from getting the help that he needs. He needs the light and he may want to walk in the light, but the addiction has become his prisoner. He is living a lie, and those closest to him are paying the price. If this is your story, let me encourage you to get some help. Come clean and turn from your sin. There are min- istries and programs that exist to walk with you and help you to overcome the sin and addiction. Don't suffer in silence.

We all need people in our lives to help us to guard our hearts and to continue to press into living honorable, trustworthy lives. Karen suggests that it is helpful to periodically ask our wives, "Does my behavior give you confidence? Do I live and respond to you in such a way that draws your trust?" Further, are there godly men in your life who can ask you direct, hard questions? When we are open, growing, and overcoming, we give our wives a sense of assurance and confidence.

"Shepherd the Flock"

The sixth gift is *leadership*. First Peter 5:2–3 says, "Shepherd the flock of God that is among you, exercising oversight, not under compulsion, but willingly, as God would have you; not for shame- ful gain, but eagerly; not domineering over those in your charge, but being examples to the flock."

The authority to lead is found in our ability to serve. This is the lesson that Jesus was teaching His disciples in John 13:1–20

when he washed their feet. Think about it. Jesus is the everlast-
ing Son of God. He created the universe, including these disciples.
And yet He got down on His knees, with a towel and a basin, and
washed their feet. This is the kind of leadership that husbands and
fathers are charged with exercising in the home.

Karen shares how I had the privilege of serving my parents.
In April of 1995, on the evening before I was scheduled to fly to
East Africa for an extended ministry trip, I received a call from my
mother. She was anxious and upset. Pop had to be hospitalized
because of complications related to his congestive heart failure.
Things didn't look good. I cancelled the trip and took a flight to
Roanoke, Virginia, to be with my parents.

Neither Mom nor Pop was doing well. Mom had just been dis-
charged from the hospital a week or so before Pop was admitted.
She had very high blood pressure and her doctor had her admitted to the hospital as a precaution, as he feared she would have a
stroke. Caring for Pop, the love and joy of her life, and watching
his health decline wore on her and was affecting her health. Seeing
him suffer elevated her blood pressure to dangerous levels. When
I arrived at the hospital and consulted with the doctors, it was
determined that in order to relieve Mom from the physical and
emotional burden of caring for Pop that it would be best to place
him in an assisted-living home.

Now, you have to know that one of the great privileges of
my life was to be able to help and assist my parents as they were
headed toward home. My sisters and I were blessed beyond measure to have parents who sacrificed and gave everything they had
to take care of us. So it was no chore. Pop was a servant-leader.
Now it was my turn.

But this was one of the most difficult things I have ever had to do in my life. Pop was strong and independent and had spent his life providing and caring for others. Now I had to tell him that he had to go to an assisted-living home. But I knew that it had to be done. I just wasn't sure how he would respond. As I stood there in his hospital room alongside his doctor and told Pop that in light of Mom's health and his needs it would be best that he be cared for at an assisted-living facility, there was a quiet, thoughtful expression on his face. Then he turned to his doctor and said, "Whatever my son says I need to do, I'll do it."

Leadership is caring and empowering others to do and be all that God has in store for them. It is not shying away from the hard, difficult challenges but stepping toward them. It is taking what has been given to us or put in our charge to steward and pouring ourselves into caring for it with a willing and a humble heart (1 Peter 5:2–3). It means that we are not passive, but we show up for our wives and take the initiative to provide loving support and direction for them and our family.

When Karen speaks about this kind of servant leadership, she points out that as women age, their demeanor and even appearance often tells the story of how they've been loved and cared for. If we want our wives to flourish and glow, then we need to give them the kind of loving leadership that lightens their load, that puts wind in their sails and joy in their hearts.

To think about . . .

What do you think are some of the things that get in the way of spouses giving each other the tenderness and support they need? How about in your marriage specifically? What could you do about it?

6

Gifts:
What Every
Husband Needs

Karen and Crawford: *Our two sons are pastors. They have planted churches and they have been called to serve and lead churches that are committed to diversity. Both Bryan and Bryndan are pioneers and have had to press in to some of the hard challenges associated with their calling. They would tell you that there have been difficult, lonely stretches along their journey. But they would also tell you that God has used their wives to bless, encourage, and strengthen them.*

Our daughters-in-law, Korie and Lucretia, are gifts from God. Besides being the mothers of six of our grandchildren, they have given themselves to our sons and supported them each step of the way. They have sacrificed in order to see the fulfillment of the vision and ministry God has called them and their husbands to. They have poured themselves into their marriages, and God is honoring their commitment.

Over time, spouses have a way of becoming more like each other. My sisters and I saw this growing up, how our parents "rubbed off" on each other. Mom was sweet and compassionate and less direct. She was not very confrontational.

On the other hand, Pop didn't beat around the bush. If you didn't want a direct, straight answer, it was probably best that you didn't ask him a question. If you didn't know him, you could think he was a bit harsh. But as they grew older, Pop became more tender and compassionate and patient; and believe it or not, Mom would surprise us with how direct and "bottom line" she could be. It was a sweet thing to watch.

Karen and I have also seen this as we have watched our children and observed the interactions and influence their spouses are having on them. We are especially impressed and at times amused at the changes we have seen in our sons. Let's just say that both of them had some "macho" tendencies when they got married. Now to see them appropriately deferring to their wives, and to witness a growing selflessness, is a joy.

Wives should never underestimate the role and power they have in influencing their husbands. I am a different man because of Karen and her *intentional* investment in my life. It is not just the gifts that she has given to me, which I will outline, but it is the gift of *herself* that is both a priceless treasure and gives me a sobering sense of accountability and responsibility. Through the years I have learned not to compete with her strengths but to learn from them, leverage them, and, yes, absorb them so that I can be a better person.

But making the kind of sacrificial investments we looked at in the last chapter, and will look at in this chapter, is not natural. It takes real dependence on the Lord and genuine humility. It is submitting to and nurturing the attitude and disposition found in Philippians 2:3–4: "Do nothing from selfish ambition or conceit, but in humility count others more significant than yourselves. Let each of you look not only to his own interests, but also to the interests of others."

So, wives, what are the foundational gifts your husband needs from you? As we mentioned in the last chapter, the greatest gift we bring and give to life and to all of our relationships is our intentional pursuit of godliness. As a wife pursues her relationship with Christ, she is experiencing His transforming power, which in turn is seen and felt by her husband and children. The fruit of the Spirit (Christlike character) found in Galatians 5:22–23 are becoming an ever-increasing reality. This is the foundation and source of power and hope of every marriage.

Beyond that greatest gift of all, what does your husband need? What encourages him and makes him feel valued and honored by the most important person in his life?

"Respectful and Pure Conduct"

The first is *respect*. First Peter 3:1–2 says, "Likewise, wives, be subject to your own husbands, so that even if some do not obey the word, they may be won without a word by the conduct of their wives, when they see your respectful and pure conduct."

Every member of the family needs and deserves to be respected. For that matter, every human being bears the image of God, and our God-given dignity deserves to be honored and respected. Our wife and children should be treated with kindness and regard for their personhood and value. The need for respect is not exclusively a male need or husband's need.

But the need for respect, although not an *exclusive* need, is a *particular* need for every husband. Dr. Emerson and Sarah Eggerichs underscore this in their excellent book, *Love and Respect.* Just as our wives have a primary need to be loved, men have a primary need to be respected. The key word is *primary*. Again, men need to be loved and women need to be respected. But for a man, a husband, his role is affirmed and validated by the gift of respect from the most important person in his life, his wife.

First Peter 3:1–2 teaches us that respect has to do with honoring your husband for his assigned place in God's order, in your life and in the home. As we said, the fact that the man is the head of the house has nothing to do with his value or worth, but for whatever reason, God has assigned him that role and place and has placed in him the need to be affirmed and honored in that assignment. No, he is not God and is, therefore, fallible and imperfect. He sometimes needs to be corrected and challenged. But he should know and feel respect from those he serves.

Years ago, Karen and I knew a woman who put her husband down at every opportunity. She criticized him publicly, everything from his parenting to his money management. It was hard to watch. And, not surprisingly, they are no longer married. If you want to emasculate a man, disregard and dishonor his leadership in the home and in the family. Compete with him for authority. Challenge him and put him down in front of others, especially the children and other family members.

Respect has a way of transforming men. Contrary to what some might think, respect has a way of making us feel our accountability and responsibility. I guess you could say that respect is a form of trust and confidence. When a man with any sense knows that his wife is inclined to give him the gift of heart cooperation, he does not want to abuse or dishonor the gift. He is less likely to dig in his heels and resist her insights. Her respect has encouraged him to feel secure and not threatened in his leadership.

"Love Their Husbands and Children"

Second, the gift of *support.* In Titus 2:4–5, older women are encouraged to "train the young women to love their husbands and
children, to be self-controlled, pure, working at home, kind, and
submissive to their own husbands, that the word of God may not
be reviled." The sense that you get from reading these words is
that wives and mothers are to give their focused commitment to
their husbands and families.

It seems as if everything in our culture is moving at warp speed.
Busyness and distraction is the order of the day. We are constantly
"connected" and interrupted via smartphones and our personal
screens. We've developed this love relationship with information
and activity. Added to this is the pressure to make ends meet
financially or needing the extra income to support the lifestyle
we've always wanted. Wives and husbands are both working outside of the home and advancing in their careers. We run out of time
and energy to fuel the relationship. Couples experience the almost
irresistible pull toward isolation. We begin to rationalize and make
assumptions about the relationship and marriage. Visited by feelings of vulnerability and insecurity, we begin to question how really important we are to each other. The question floats around
our minds, "In a crunch, can I count on the heart support from
my spouse?"

Men need to know that no matter what, their wives are completely there for them and will do all they can to see them through.
A man needs to know that there is one person in the world who
is *with* him, and that's his wife. In the movie *Rocky IV*, against his

wife, Adrian's, protests, Rocky travels to Russia to fight Ivan Drago. But Rocky seems distracted and not able to fully give himself to training for the fight. He misses his wife. They'd been through everything together, and she was always in his corner. One morning after a run, he returns to the cabin, and to his amazement, he sees Adrian waiting for him on the porch. That's all the motivation he needs.

Support does not mean blind allegiance or that you don't try to convince your husband to change his mind about what you think is either a bad decision or a poor course of action. In fact, if you love him, you will try to help him stay away from walking down paths that will end up at the wrong place. But even if he does make some wrong decisions you are not going to bail on him. He knows that you are with him for better or for worse. (It's easy to support him during the "better" seasons in your marriage, but it's another thing to support him during the "worse" sections of the journey.) Your husband needs to know that your support is unconditional. When we said, "I do" we were saying that sink or swim, we're in this thing together. What happens to one happens to both of us.

> A man needs to know that there is one person in the world who is *with* him, and that's his wife.

You can imagine that after forty-seven years of marriage I have my share of failures and "bonehead" decisions. Like the time early in our marriage when money was tight and I bought another car against Karen's wishes. It was a lemon and cost us money that we didn't have. We paid more money in repairs than the car was worth. Did Karen remind me that if I had listened to her we wouldn't have had to go through the hassle and pain? The short answer is yes. At no time, however, did I ever question whether she was with me. There are dozens of other stories I could share with you that underscore the depths of her love and support for me despite my wrong assumptions and decisions.

As in the case of respect, over time the gift of support has a way of making most men feel accountable and creates a desire to not want to hurt or disappoint the most important person in his life—you. It is because you support your husband that he will not want to take that gift for granted. Your demonstrated support makes him feel secure and gives him a sense of confidence and the foundation for courageous action. He doesn't feel as if he has to prove his "manhood." Your support also causes him to be less defensive and more teachable.

"Working at Home, Kind"

Third, the gift of *encouragement*. The instructions in Titus 2:4–5 suggest that wives and mothers should create an environment of encouragement in the home.

Life is unpredictable and filled with surprises, and not always good ones. The tragic twists and turns of life can leave us reeling and drain us of hope, confidence, and courage. We can leave the house in the morning filled with joy and the expectation of a great day only to return home in the evening with our heads drooping and our shoulders slumped. The day didn't go according to expectations. All of us can identify. During those times, we need fresh wind in our sails. Everybody needs encouragement. If a person has a pulse, they need encouragement. Every member of your family needs encouragement. Wives need it. Children need it. Husbands need it.

To encourage literally means to *give courage*. Although the gift of support and encouragement are related, I tend to think of encouragement as more specific words and expressions or intentional actions to lift someone's spirits. Words are powerful. They can kill and damage, or they can give life and hope. I'm not sure if men need more encouragement than women, but we definitely need to be given the gift of encouragement from our life partner.

A man needs to know that not only is his wife on his team but that she is proud of him and affirms his commitment to love and care for his family. He may not have an impressive job or occupation, but he is doing the best he can to fulfill his responsibilities and obligations. He needs to know that his wife values who he is and what he is doing. This is particularly true during hard, challenging times. The right words can make all of the difference in the world. When bad news or feelings of inadequacy and disappointment visit your husband, he needs the assurance that the one he has committed himself to is there to cheer him on.

I was visiting my parents about a year or so before Pop died. As I walked into the kitchen, I heard my father complaining to my mother about something she did or didn't do that he was upset about. It was a relatively minor thing and, frankly, I thought Pop was a little over the top. But he wouldn't let it go. When he finished his speech, my mother looked him in the eye and said, "I just want you to remember that we're all we got." Pop was embarrassed. He lowered his head and said, "You're right, Sylvia, we're all we got." It dawned on him that for more than fifty years they had been there for each other and picked each other up when they were down. When they couldn't rely on others for words of affirmation and encouragement, they could always turn to each other.

Marriage should be characterized by mutual encouragement. Karen knows that my primary love language is words of encouragement. She is my constant cheerleader. She senses when I need a word of affirmation or when I've had a tough day. She can tell by the sound of my voice and body language if I am a bit down or weary. Sometimes the encouragement comes from a touch or a knowing smile. Often God uses her encouragement to give me perspective and to lighten the load. Both of us have made a conscious commitment to say something encouraging to each other every day. If we don't do it, who will?

Does your husband need to be encouraged? Does he feel valued and appreciated? Have you told him lately that you're proud of him? Does he know that you're praying for him and his specific needs and challenges?

"A Man Shall . . . Hold Fast to His Wife"

The fourth gift is *loyalty*. To be loyal is to give your allegiance to a person or an institution. Let's look again at those words in Genesis 2:24: "Therefore a man shall leave his father and mother and *hold fast* to his wife, and they shall become one flesh" (emphasis added). When God spoke these words to Adam, He was defining the nature and meaning of marriage. Again, notice the words "hold fast." As we have said, to hold fast implies that the marriage is the priority relationship in all of life. We have an exclusive relationship that is defined by love and loyalty.

Again, there is a relationship between support, encouragement, and loyalty. But, specifically, loyalty says that there is never any question as to whose team you're on and who you are committed to (Gen. 2:24). To your husband this means at least two things.

• It means your commitment to him as your husband will not be trespassed or violated by any other relationship. What he thinks and feels is to be considered first. No, this doesn't mean that he is always right or that as a couple you should not get the advice and counsel of others. But it does mean that you two are the first and primary team. You don't allow others to sabotage or dismantle the love and commitment you have to and for each other.

• Loyalty also means that you will not pull back or abandon your husband during hard or challenging times or when he makes a decision that you disagree with (even if you are right). It's relatively easy to be loyal when there is agreement and when life is predictable. Everybody is comfortable. But loyalty is challenged, proved, and strengthened when we are called to make a sacrifice. In fact, we know that we are loyal *because* our commitment has been challenged and tested. We push aside our preferences for the sake of our vows.

Karen is not big on change. She likes routine. She would have loved to have stayed in the Philadelphia area for the rest of her life. But she married me. Through the years there have been significant changes in our lives. We lived in the Philadelphia area where I served as an evangelist for a Christian organization. We lived in Dallas, Texas, for two years where I served as a church planter. We moved to Atlanta when we joined the staff of Cru (formerly Campus Crusade for Christ). Then in 2005 I became the senior pastor of Fellowship Bible Church. All these major changes required Karen to adjust.

In addition, there have been other surprises thrown at us, calling us, and particularly Karen, to walk away from the comfort of the predictable in order to support what I believed the Lord was leading us to do. I cannot begin to describe the depths of Karen's loyalty and commitment to me. Her sacrifices through the years are in the trophy case of my heart. She is my rock.

"Whoever Restrains His Lips Is Prudent"

The fifth gift is *confidentiality*. Proverbs 31 describes the woman who fears the Lord. Take a look at verses 11 and 12: "The heart of her husband trusts in her, and he will have no lack of gain. She does him good, and not harm, all the days of her life." Then there's Proverbs 10:19: "When words are many, transgression is not lacking, but whoever restrains his lips is prudent."

Notice that the Proverbs 31 woman has captured the trust and confidence of her husband, and in Proverbs 10:19 we are cautioned to exercise discipline and restraint when we speak. When we put them together, the message is that we should live in such a way that we can be trusted with information. We are careful with what we say and to whom we say it. Husbands need to know that what we share with our wives is kept between us.

Yes, every couple needs safe people in their lives, people who have proved that they can be trusted. We need mentors and counselors to help us sort through the issues and challenges we face as couples. We need them to help us with perspective, to help us heal and overcome our wounds. We need them to pray with us and for us and to be available. They are God's special gifts and expressions of His love for us. As couples, we have agreed and given these people access to privileged information about our lives and the issues in the relationship. The point is that *together* we have invited them in.

Unless there is mutual agreement, couples should protect

**Intimacy means
that there are
things that are just
between us and
that no one else
should know.**

their business and not make it anyone else's. One of the fastest ways to destroy trust is to share information without permission or to betray confidences. To be sure, there are some exceptions—say, abuse, dysfunction, or something illegal or unethical going on in the relationship. That information needs to be shared with those who can help. But here we're talking about sharing information with friends or other people without the consent of your spouse.

Think about it. Intimacy means that there are things that are just between us and that no one else should know. It is not just that it is privileged information. No one should know your husband or information about your husband and marriage to the degree you do. Because of this, it is wise to discuss with each other what can be shared with others and what shouldn't be shared. When in doubt, don't. Karen and I don't share private matters unless we give each other permission. When we talk about sensitive things, we assume it's just between us. Husbands and wives need to give each other the gift of confidentiality. But in a particular sense, a man has a need to be assured that his words and trust is safe with the woman he has committed his life to.

Now in a marriage, we aren't always going to agree on all this or a lot of other things. But what does it mean to deal with each other's differences, resolve conflict, and learn forgiveness? Read on . . .

To think about . . .

Why do you think the author names "keeping confidences" as an issue especially important to men?

What does it look like for a wife to support a husband through failure or poor decisions?

7

How Two Imperfect People Resolve Conflict

Karen: *One of the reasons why I shied away from conflict in the early years of our marriage is because of the constant conflict between my mother and stepfather. At times it got completely out of hand. They yelled and screamed at each other, and a few times they got physical. Then there were those times in which they ignored each other, freezing the other out with the silent treatment.*

What made matters worse was that my mother kept inviting her father into the affairs of their marriage. I remember this terrible argument they had about the purchase of a Boy Scout uniform for my brother. Mom had gone directly to her father and asked him to buy the uniform without saying a word to my stepfather. He felt disrespected, and late one evening he exploded. I remember shaking with fear. The constant tension between them and their inability to respect and honor each other affected me.

Not every marriage is going to face the conflict Karen's mother and stepfather struggled with. But be assured, you *will* have conflict at some point. It's inevitable. Why? Well, first, we can be drawn to the "differentness" of another person. We admire traits in them we wish we had. For example, an introvert may be drawn to an extrovert who is at ease around and draws energy from people. Or an extrovert may be drawn to an introvert because they seem to be so at home with solitude or relating to a small group of trusted friends.

Or maybe we fall in love with someone whose background and family is completely different than what we've known and experienced. There is the tendency to minimize the differences because, after all, we love each other and that's all that matters, isn't it? Then after the honeymoon, reality sets in.

Then, of course, there's the obvious (or at least should be) reality that no two people are exactly alike. If you have more than one child, no doubt you're nodding your head in agreement. My sisters and I have different personalities, and we don't always think the same way about life, interests, and issues. So when a young engaged couple sit across from me and happily state, "We have so much in common and we are alike in so many ways," I am tempted to tell them the truth: "You're about to discover that there are a lot more differences than you realize."

So we need to expect and assume that we will experience conflict in marriage. That isn't easy to hear. Some of us will avoid conflict at all costs. We are peacekeepers, and we view disagreement as either some sort of rejection or damaging the unity of the marriage.

To be sure, none of us should like conflict or be contentious. But neither should we always avoid it. Conflict can actually be constructive, leading to meaningful change and a deeper, sweeter intimacy in your relationship. It all depends on how we handle it and what happens as result of the conflict.

Think about it. Part of what makes a relationship rich and

meaningful is that you've worked through
difficulties and disagreements. You value
the relationship, so you press through the
challenges and conflicts. Again, conflict tests
our commitment. Leaving, holding fast,
and becoming one flesh (Gen. 2:24) can be
painful and requires a degree of grit and

> We want to leave
> a legacy of what it
> means to forgive,
> resolve issues,
> and deal with our
> differences.

determination. When we get close to each other, it's difficult to
escape or ignore the things we don't like or that irritate us. But
we're all in. And since there is no such thing as a conflict-free
relationship, we commit ourselves to addressing and resolving any
and every issue that stands in the way of pursuing and experiencing oneness.

In addition, because marriage is meant to influence and shape
future generations, we want to leave a legacy of what it means to
forgive, resolve issues, and deal with our differences. This tells the
truth about God and the power of the gospel in our marriage. But
this kind of heart loyalty is becoming increasingly uncommon. We
live in a culture where commitment is relative and people walk
away from marriage as if they were changing jobs.

Conflict separates us and divides us as couples—contrary to
God's desire for unity ("one flesh") in marriage. When there is
something between us, a barrier is erected that says, "This is as far
as you're going to get." We have to figure out how to remove the
barrier, bring warmth and openness back to the relationship, and
get back on the path to "becoming one."

Karen and I have had our share of conflict. As you have seen,
we are very different in many ways and we both have strong
personalities. At times this has made for some choppy waters.

Added to this, our personalities and backgrounds cause us to approach conflict differently. For example, Karen tends to be less direct and will want to take a bit more time addressing the conflict. I tend to be more direct and want to get things resolved quickly. You can imagine this has caused some problems. But we have learned through the years to adjust to each other and to appreciate how the other person responds.

Again: *If we want a marriage that not only goes the distance and is characterized by rich, sweet intimacy but also serves as a model of hope and encouragement for future generations, we have to commit ourselves to dealing with and resolving conflict.*

Here are some of the lessons we've learned.

Accept the reality that we are flawed.

Psalm 51:5 says, "Behold, I was brought forth in iniquity, and in sin did my mother conceive me." Romans 3:23 says, "For *all* have sinned and fall short of the glory of God" (emphasis added).

If you married a human being, you married a sinner. There have never been and never will be any perfect, sinless people available. We are sinners and will bring our sin nature into the marriage. Certainly we should be intentional about overcoming our sin and shortcomings and not make excuses for selfishness, hurtful actions and responses, and poor behavior in general. We should never accommodate sin but face it and deal with it through heartfelt repentance.

But sin is pervasive. We sin and we have been affected by the sins of others. When a teenager decides to have sex and gets pregnant and then has to raise that child as a single parent, she then has to live with the repercussions and consequences of her sinful decision. Her choice didn't just affect her, it impacts the child and spills over into an ever-widening circle of influence. When a person grows up in a home where abuse, arguments, and demeaning and dismissive language filled the atmosphere, they are often scarred in ways they're not aware of. Sometimes it takes years to fully realize and recognize the negative impact.

Then there's the stuff in us simply because we are the children of Adam. We don't need negative influences or examples to sin. We sin because it is the natural thing for us to do. It is in us. We're drawn to it, and as long as we are alive, we will be tempted and will fight the battle to get better and to overcome sin.

Perhaps you're engaged and these words strike you as being a bit negative and strong. You may even be thinking, "Yeah, I get the whole idea of sin, but my fiancé, although not perfect, doesn't appear to be as sinful as others."

To be sure, there are varying degrees of the expression of our sinfulness—but make no mistake about it: the sweetest, kindest person in the world has the capacity to do awful things. In addition, selfishness is in all of us. Some of us may not think of ourselves as selfish or be characterized as such, but if you probe deep enough, you will find it.

The nature of marriage has a way of magnifying our sinfulness and, especially, putting the spotlight on our selfishness. Once we say "I do" and begin living with each other and occupying the same space, the rose-colored glasses are removed and what we perhaps ignored or minimized about each other is now an inescapable reality. As we said early on in the book, the struggle to change each other sets in. If we're not careful, we can become guilty of recognizing the sin and failures of our spouse and ignoring our own stuff. We get backed into a hypocrisy that can erect an almost impenetrable barrier, making conflict resolution impossible.

During the early days of our marriage, both Karen and I had a hard time admitting that we were wrong. I felt, probably more than she did, that I had to project this aura of perfection. Now I fully knew that I wasn't perfect or close to it. But somewhere along the line, I bought into this notion that to be the head of my household meant that I had to be perceived as always being "right," somehow less needy. But that was nothing more than insecurity cloaked in a false spirituality. In a word, pride. Further, keeping up this notion of being "flawless" or not as needy began to crumble. It wasn't sustainable because it wasn't the truth.

Enduring love is not based on perfection or performance. Enduring love is unconditional acceptance. It says that if we are going to overcome the issues, challenges, and the inevitable disagreements and conflicts we will have, then we have to shed the pretense, to acknowledge that we both come from imperfect backgrounds and carry in us and with us the scars of sin and the propensity to sin.

But this kind of love is anchored in humility. It says that we are dependent on God and we need His grace, mercy, and help to be what we were born to be. This humility also says that we need each other to get to where we should. We then address the conflict as imperfect people who want to get better. Not as those who have arrived.

Silence doesn't solve anything.

We have also learned that, typically, silence doesn't solve problems or resolve conflicts. Ephesians 4:26–27 says, "Be angry and do not sin; *do not let the sun go down on your anger*, and give no opportunity to the devil" (emphasis added). Galatians 6:1 says, "If anyone is caught in any transgression, you who are spiritual should *restore him in a spirit of gentleness*" (emphasis added). Matthew 18:15: "If your brother sins against you, *go* and tell him his fault" (emphasis added).

Then Matthew 5:23–24 says, "So if you are offering your gift at the altar and there remember that your brother has something against you, *leave your gift there before the altar and go. First be reconciled to your brother*, and then come and offer your gift" (emphasis added). These passages teach us that we're not to be passive about conflict. We're to do something about it.

I used to believe that some people just don't deal with conflict. They avoid it at all costs, and they think that because they don't face it head-on that somehow it will go away. Nonengagement will keep them from having to confront unpleasant issues, and that means that they will not be affected.

But this is not true. Everybody is affected by conflict and responds to it. We will either be intentional or passive, meaning we will either deal with it directly or indirectly.

Karen and I know of a young couple whose marriage, as of this writing, is in trouble. When the couple has a conflict, the husband withdraws and refuses to engage. Instead of expressing his feelings and thoughts, he resorts to silence and angry, reactive behavior. You know that he has been hurt or offended, but he can't or won't bring himself to face the issue. In his mind, he may be thinking that he is avoiding the discomfort of dealing with disagreement. But in fact, his passive-aggressive behavior is evidence that he is dealing with the conflict and not in a good way. Sadly, he is not willing to get help.

We have found that most people fall into two broad categories when it comes to responding to conflict: those who are more direct and inclined to face conflict; and, as we have seen, those who are more indirect and inclined not to face it head-on.

Obviously, there is a spectrum in each of these categories. In our marriage, I tend to be the one who is more inclined to want to deal with it directly and get it settled. Karen has a tendency to want to think it through and talk about it later. In her words, at times she will "stuff" her feelings for a while. On the other hand, my impatience has caused me to say too much and act too quickly. The better part of wisdom would have been to take a step back and get a better perspective. God has used our different "styles" to temper us and help us appreciate and understand how the other person responds.

If you shrink from conflict . . .

Karen shares that she has learned that stuffing her feelings is not a good thing. It can do more harm than intended. It's not helpful to run away from an issue, sulk in a corner, or walk away angry. Again, because conflict is a given, we have to learn how to face it and work through it. She offers these suggestions to those who may have a tendency to shrink back from conflict.

First, conflict is best addressed in a climate of love and acceptance. This is particularly true for the person who is not inclined to deal with conflict directly. They need to be assured that the issue is the issue and *they* are not the issue. As a couple, *you* need to be a safe place to discuss issues. Love and mutual affirmation go a long way in keeping the communication lines open.

Second, resist the temptation to walk away, change the subject, or emotionally disconnect. If you need more time to be prepared to address the issue, then choose an agreed upon-time and follow through.

Third, keep your insecurities in check. Don't posture yourself as if you're looking for a fight. When we are defensive, it's as if we brought a portable wall to the conversation. We're saying, "I'm hearing your words but I'm not moving and you're really not going to get through." Instead, our attitude and posture should communicate a willingness to listen and to give thoughtful consideration to what is being said.

Fourth, talk. Calmly express your feelings and thoughts. Don't assume that your spouse knows how you feel or even what you think, even though he/she *should* know. Work on learning how to express yourself. You may have to write down your thoughts and feelings and read them.

Choose what offends you.

We have also learned that we have to choose what offends us. "Choosing what offends us" may sound a bit odd. After all, we are who we are and we can't just decide or determine what offends us, can we? The short answer is yes. As the saying goes, we have to pick our battles, decide what are the issues worth addressing, and what are the things that we simply have to let go. If we decided to address everything that we don't like or speak to all of the stuff that we disagree with or linger over a hurtful comment, life would come to a standstill and, frankly, so would our maturity.

We're not suggesting that we adopt some hard-nosed, suck-it-up-and-get-over-it attitude toward each other. *Anything* that stands in the way of pursuing oneness in the relationship should be addressed and resolved. But it's also important to keep in mind that love gives the benefit of the doubt. First Corinthians 13:5 says that love "is not irritable or resentful." This means that love should not be fragile and easily offended.

> Your husband or wife can be 90 percent incredible. But then there's that 10 percent that you just can't stand.

There's a certain security and stability that comes with love. This helps us to develop perspective and proportion when our spouse does or says something that we don't like. Because we love them, we think before we respond. We ask ourselves, "Should I be offended by this? Is this something that I can let go? What difference will this issue make in a month, a year, or even ten years from now?"

We have a tendency to magnify the weaknesses in our spouse. Your husband or wife can be 90 percent incredible. But then there's that 10 percent that you just can't stand. We tend to isolate the 10 percent and not see it in proportion or relationship to the 90 percent. Granted, that 10 percent could be a big deal . . . but maybe not. We just need to be careful that we don't get petty and picky and lose sight of the weightier, more significant issues in the relationship. Do we really want to spend a lot of emotional energy and capital arguing over not hanging up the towels the "right way"?

Karen used to get irritated with me when I came home from a trip and didn't unpack my suitcases right away. This bugged her to no end, and believe me, she'd let me know about it. Then she stopped "reminding" me about it. I was curious as to why she stopped, so I asked her. She said she decided that in the scheme of things this was not a big deal and she just needed to let it go. Actually, her response encouraged me to unpack my suitcases when I got home!

The reality is that there is always something to fight about. Let's prioritize the issues, extend grace to each other, and build a tolerance for the nonessential stuff. Let's think about what we really need to work on and resolve.

Cultivate trust and transparency.

We have learned that trust and transparency gives us the confidence to address issues. Charles Dickens said, "Never close your lips to those to whom you have opened your heart." Marriage is all about giving the gift of trust and honoring the trust that has been given to us. When we exchanged vows, we entered into an exclusive relationship and committed ourselves to both being one and becoming one. There's no one else in the world that we will have this kind of intimate relationship with. And that's the way it was intended to be. It is assumed that the person we have committed our lives to can be trusted.

Trust is the foundation for transparency. After God brought Adam and Eve together, Genesis 2:25 tells us, "And the man and his wife were both naked and were not ashamed." They were together and they had nothing to hide. There was no question as to whether or not they would trust each other. They were made for each other and they had given themselves to each other. Thus, there were no walls, barriers, or anything hidden from each other. This is what marriage is intended to be and what every couple should pursue in their relationship. Openness. Vulnerability. A safe place.

Some of us pull back from addressing and resolving conflict because trust has been eroded in us and we feel as if we have no choice but to protect ourselves. This was the case with Karen. In the early years of our marriage, when we would have a conflict, I found myself reassuring her of my love and commitment. She came from a background where divorce and broken relationships were the rule and not the exception. And increasingly this is the legacy that's been placed in the hands of so many couples.

Many of us are guarded because we don't want to be hurt and we are uncertain about our spouse's exclusive, heart commitment to us. Our defenses are up and we find it hard to trust and to be open. The uncertainty and insecurity makes it very difficult to press into disagreements. Somehow the curtain has to be pulled back and heavy doses of unconditional love and trustworthy behavior poured over the relationship in order to wash away the fear and insecurity. This builds trust and confidence in the relationship that leads to transparency.

Then, when we have to address issues or resolve conflict, the question of love and commitment is not on the table but the issue is. We can share and interact with confidence because we know that we have given each other our hearts. First John 4:18 says, "There is no fear in love, but perfect love casts out fear."

Is your marriage characterized by trust and transparency? Would your spouse say that they can share with you who they really are and what they are thinking without fear of rejection? Can they trust you with their feelings and say even hard things to you without questioning your love and commitment to them or you questioning their love and commitment to you?

Remember that forgiveness is the path to resolution.

We have learned that forgiveness is the path to resolution. At the core of conflict is an offense. Someone is hurt or angry. An expectation has not been met. Someone has been overlooked or ignored. Perhaps harsh or inappropriate words have been spoken. Promises have not been kept. There are many ways in which we can offend our spouse and they can offend us. But one thing is for sure: resolving conflict requires the ability to give and receive forgiveness.

I realize that we've touched on forgiveness already. But it is a big deal. In fact, one of the first questions I ask couples that are thinking about getting married has to do with their ability to forgive. There can be no authenticity in any relationship without committing to and becoming proficient in forgiving and being forgiven. Further, conflict cannot be resolved apart from saying the words, "I was wrong. Will you forgive me?" And then the person who is offended saying, "I forgive you." This takes humility, the ability to swallow our pride.

Every time we face a disagreement with our spouse we have to own the reality that one of us may be wrong. And if it is me, then I'm deciding beforehand to ask for forgiveness. If I am right there's no purpose or value in gloating. The relationship is more important than the issue. So if I am right I need to humbly extend forgiveness, fully realizing that my turn to be wrong is just around the corner. As we've said, pretense and the aura of perfection is the enemy to intimacy. It creates an impenetrable façade that leaves us isolated and drains the joy out of the marriage.

Forgiveness is an act and an attitude. Look again at Ephesians 4:32, "Be kind to one another, tenderhearted, forgiving one another, as God in Christ forgave you." Notice that the act of forgiving is in the context of *kindness* and *tenderheartedness*. The demeanor of kindness and tenderness should permeate the marriage. This demonstrated care and affection for each other makes it easier to give and receive forgiveness. In other words, it is the norm of the relationship to express love, understanding, and grace toward each other.

So when we have to discuss and resolve a conflict, it is in the context of love and security. We know that even if we are the one who's wrong, our spouse does not reject us. There's help and forgiveness. Forgiveness releases God's rich, wonderful grace into the marriage. Forgiveness has a way of washing away defensiveness. It says, "I love you anyway."

Forgiveness declares that we are not enemies, we are allies.

These days Karen and I are quicker to apologize and ask for forgiveness from each other. During these forty-seven years we have been through a lot and we have had a front-row seat for the work of God's amazing grace in each other's lives and in our marriage. By God's grace we have faced some hard things and worked through differences. We have had to face our imperfections and shortcomings. We have come to the conclusion that one of the greatest gifts we can place in the hands of our children and grandchildren is the legacy of forgiveness. We want them to know that during hard, difficult times in a marriage, you don't turn on each other or attack each other, but you turn toward each other with open arms and the willingness to forgive. Forgiveness declares that we are not enemies, we are allies.

Take direct action to resolve conflict.

We have learned that in order to resolve conflict, we have to take clear, direct, specific action. Identifying the issue and talking through the conflict/offense is wonderful. Expressing and receiving forgiveness is very important. But the question is what are we going to *do* to overcome the problem or resolve the issue, especially if it threatens the oneness in the relationship? Nothing is more frustrating than having the same conversation over and over and there is no movement toward solution or development. Procrastination or the lack of meaningful action fuels indifference and resentment.

I have known of couples that have gotten "stuck" in their marriage. The problem isn't that they don't know what the problem is or that they have not discussed it many times. They've even gone to counseling, read books in the area that they are struggling with, and gone to marriage conferences and retreats. It's almost as if they want someone to be their surrogate will, doing the work that only they can do. Information, content, and accurate, spot-on advice and insight have never changed anyone's life or even improved a marriage. Meaningful change takes place when we implement and execute a course of action.

Karen and I have found it helpful to determine *before* we address a conflict that we not only need to find a solution but we are going to identify what we need to do to make it right. Then after we hear each other out we ask, "What should we do about this?" Or if one of us needs to change, the question is, "What should I do about this?" We may have to think about the best way of moving forward and come back with a course of action later. Depending on the nature of the conflict, we may need to seek the advice and insight of a trusted friend or counselor. But action is required. Our love for each other and the value we place on our marriage is seen through what we do to remove the barriers to oneness and intimacy.

As we've said, there is no such thing as a conflict-free marriage. To be married means to experience conflict. Conflict in itself is

How we face our differences and work through them will, to a large degree, determine the condition of what we place in the hands of future generations.

not the issue. The important thing is how we approach it and what we do about it. God allows us to experience conflict to express His grace and mercy, to change us and make us more like Jesus, and to deepen and enrich our love and commitment to each other.

How we face our differences and work through them will, to a large degree, determine the condition and shape of what we place in the hands of future generations. We want them to be filled with hope and encouragement. We want them to look back and see that we didn't ignore or deny our "stuff" or turn on one another. We faced the challenges and issues and turned toward each other and toward our great God . . . and did He ever help us!

To think about . . .

Do you agree with the author that if you probe deep enough, we're all selfish? Can you think of an instance from your own life?

Do you and your spouse argue about the same things over and over? How could you break this pattern?

The Great Handoff

Karen: *I didn't grow up in a home where Christ-centered living was modeled before me. That's why I am so grateful for my church family that loved me, and the couples and families who were inviting examples of what it looks like to have a godly marriage and home. They served as my spiritual parents and placed in my hands what I longed for and needed. They didn't give me formal "lessons" on how to be a Christian wife and mother; I just watched them and absorbed what I saw. Not only did their example help to prepare me to be a godly wife and mother but also how to be Crawford's partner in ministry.*

For example, Pastor Kowalchuk (Pastor K) and his wife, Vera, left their Russian-speaking church to lead our small church with a declining membership and changing demographics. Mrs. K never complained but rolled up her sleeves and embraced this new challenge—and us. She hosted our youth group. She modeled hospitality and etiquette. She had a quiet strength and at the same time she honored her husband. This left a lasting impression on me. God used her and other families in the church to give me hope and confidence that God could do the same for me and through me.

O ne of our favorite stories is the moving tribute that Gregory Hines paid to the legendary entertainer Sammy Davis Jr. Davis was a mentor and father figure to dancer-actor Hines. Hines shared how Davis supported his career and opened doors for him. He was always there for him.

Davis was stricken with throat cancer and began to rapidly deteriorate. Hines, realizing that time was short, went to see his dear mentor and friend. When he walked into the house, he saw Davis sitting on a couch. He was shocked by how frail and weak he had become. Hines sat down and shared with Davis how much he had meant to him and that he loved him. It was a tearful, bittersweet visit. Hines got up and began walking toward the front door. But then he heard the sound of shuffling feet. He turned around and to his amazement there was Sammy Davis Jr. standing in front of him, holding an imaginary basketball. Davis looked Hines in the eye and passed him the ball. Hines got the message. Sammy Davis Jr. died two weeks later.

What are we placing in the hands of future generations? As we've said, what we believe, what we do, and who we are have far-reaching implications. This was God's plan from the very beginning.

But this "handoff" is not a once-and-for-all event. As parents and spouses we're doing this on a daily basis. And there are those milestones in the lives of our children that push us toward reflection. When we drop our child off for the first day of school, the questions swirl in your mind. Will they remember what we taught them about sharing and getting along with others? When they enter middle school and high school: Will they remember what we taught them about making good choices and decisions? What about when we drop them off at college? Have we nurtured them and prepared them so that they know what they believe and why they believe it? And will they be faithful in their walk and relationship with the Lord?

And then there's that conversation: "Mom and Dad, I want to talk to you. I've fallen in love and I believe this is the one. We want to get married and spend the rest of our lives together." You make sure they go through premarital counseling and are exposed to the resources that can help them start on the right foot. You're there on their wedding day filled with joy. But you wonder: Have we modeled before them and placed in their hands what is eternally important and significant?

Karen and I have been there. It felt as if we were passing them the baton in a relay race. Are they prepared to run their leg of the race?

There are constant challenges facing every couple, threatening to minimize, divert, or destroy their oneness and the mission of marriage. Different backgrounds. Personal struggles. Unanticipated adversity. The work and attacks of our enemy, the devil. The list is endless. So what do we do to lay a foundation of hope and confidence for the next generation?

"So That They Should Set Their Hope in God"

Psalm 78:5–7 gives us direction. Admittedly, this is not specifically a passage on marriage, but it is about the stewardship of the mission of the family from one generation to the next. Look closely at these words. "He established a testimony in Jacob and appointed a law in Israel, which he commanded our fathers to teach to their children, that the next generation might know them, the children yet unborn, and arise and tell them to their children, *so that they should set their hope in God and not forget the works of God, but keep his commandments*" (emphasis added).

In Psalm 78 Asaph is reminding the Israelites (God's family) of God's unfailing faithfulness throughout their history. Despite their inconsistencies and seasons of disobedience, God has never let them down. He has provided for them, delivered them, and met their every need. God's faithfulness is their treasure and was meant to be their North Star, their point of reference, their anchor and accountability. What God has done should inspire gratitude and a desire to honor Him by living faithful, obedient lives.

Now back to verses 5–7. By way of application, these verses point us to our stewardship concerning what God has placed in our hands and what we are to place in the hands of the next generation. Nothing is more important.

It is wonderful to give our children great experiences, special family traditions and memories, a good education, a leg up in advancing in their careers. It warms our hearts to see them accomplish their goals and to witness the fulfillment of some of their dreams. But if they do not embrace and pursue what the psalmist calls us to, whatever else they do and accomplish in life will fall short of what they were born for. They will have missed the joy and soul-enriching satisfaction of having experienced the intervention and power of our living God during their moment in history. Their marriage and family will be a pedestrian reflection of the times in which they lived. What they will pass on will be memories devoid of supernatural power and presence and a sense of noble mission. Over time the memories will fade away. What's left?

Let's take a closer look at these verses. The message is clear: this has to be done. How? The psalmist outlines for us a passionate priority, a process, and a finished product.

First, we are to embrace a *passionate priority*. Verse 5 says, "He established a *testimony* . . . and appointed a *law*" (emphasis added). *Testimony* is a reference to the character of God. *Law* is a reference to the Word of God. As couples, we have to make both the decision and commitment that our lives will be marked and ordered around who God is and the celebration of His loving care, faithfulness, and intervention on our behalf.

We also revere and submit to the Word of God. The expression "appointed a law" points us to objective accountability. God's Word never changes. It expresses His love and plan for our lives. It gives us direction, perspective, wisdom, encouragement, and answers to the issues and complexities of life. The Bible is not simply a collection of inspirational material and compelling short stories given to warm our hearts and to give us moral lessons. It is the very Word of God to be believed, honored, and obeyed. God has spoken and is speaking through His Word. When He speaks, He expects us to respond.

God's character and His Word should be the theme of our households. We shouldn't be conflicted about what matters most to us. Neither should our children. And this is the foundation for future generations and what we are placing in their hands.

"Arise and tell"

But there is also a *process* the psalmist alludes to in the second part of verse 5 through verse 6: "which he commanded our fathers to teach to their children, that the next generation might know them, the children yet unborn, and arise and tell them to their children."

The word *teach* here comes from a word that means "to make known by all possible means." It has to do with not just talking about God's truth and faithfulness, but applying and integrating God's truth and what we know about His character to every area of life. This was God's message to the Israelites in Deuteronomy 6:6–9 as they were preparing to enter the Promised Land:

> And these words that I command you today shall be on your heart. You shall teach them diligently to your children, and shall talk of them when you sit in your house, and when you walk by the way, and when you lie down, and when you rise. You shall bind them as a sign on your hand, and they shall be as frontlets between your eyes. You shall write them on the doorposts of your house and on your gates.

The message is that exposure to the application of the Word of God is what our family does. Our aspiration is that everyone in our household will be infused with and marked by God's truth and His character. No, we're not suggesting that we become like Pharisees and gracelessly and hypocritically beat people up with the Bible. But with authentic, tender, compassionate, grace-filled hearts we intentionally live God's truth before our children and apply God's truth to every challenge they face. And we're not casual about this. Because this is indeed what matters most, we are intentional. This is our legacy.

We had a routine in our home. Every evening after dinner we would have family devotions. I would read a passage from the Bible and I'd ask age-appropriate questions about the text. Then Karen would bring out the notebook where we would record our prayer requests and the answers to those prayers. We prayed for people we knew. We prayed for our own needs. Whether it was for healing for an illness, making a team at school, doing well on a test, personal struggles, finances, God's direction and wisdom . . . we brought these things to the Lord in prayer. We spent individual time with our kids, sharing God's Word and praying together.

Then there were those informal, teachable moments in which the door was open to share how the Scriptures related to what they were going through or faced with. Often we would pause to celebrate God's faithfulness in answering prayer or meeting a need.

Karen and I felt that the spiritual development of our children was our responsibility. We needed to model before them and teach them what was most important. We couldn't expect that the church or Christian school would do this for us. Of course they can help, but the calling to shape these lives has been placed in our hands.

Yes, it takes time and commitment to do this. And that's the challenge, isn't it? Believe me, this wasn't always easy for us either. Everybody in the family is busy. It seems that because we don't want to miss out on anything, we are shortchanging what's most important and our attention is being diverted away from what really matters. Sometimes we just have to do less in order to do more of the right, core things.

The psalmist puts the spotlight on our motivation: "that the next generation might know them . . . and arise and tell them to their children" (v. 6). We are intentional not only about placing this eternal, transformative treasure in the hands and hearts of our children, we have a vision that every generation will faithfully walk with God. Our eyes and our hearts are on a time that we cannot see.

"Son, These People Paid Our Tuition"

A few years ago our oldest son, Bryan, and I were speaking at a conference in Asheville, NC. One afternoon we drove over to

Conover, NC, about an hour away. Conover is where my dad was born and raised. We hadn't been there since Bryan was a little boy. The memories flooded my mind as we turned onto the street where the family home once stood. We drove by where my uncles and their families used to live. Sweet memories of family reunions and laughing and playing with my cousins when I was a little boy warmed my heart.

Then we pulled up to our church, Thomas Chapel. This is a special place. This little church had served as a spiritual anchor for our family. It represented hope, encouragement, and love. Bryan and I got out of the car and walked through the cemetery behind the church where many of our family members are buried. As we read the grave markers, I reminded Bryan who these people were. We searched for Peter's grave, my great-grandfather and the former slave. We couldn't find it. We stood at the gravesite of my grandparents, Milton and Anna Loritts. We visited the graves of aunts and uncles. I knew them and shared some of their stories with my son. They were humble people who loved the Lord and whose lives in large part had been nurtured and shaped by the word of God and His faithfulness.

I was ambushed by emotion. I began to weep. I said to Bryan, "Son, these people paid our tuition." As we stood in that cemetery our minds became uncluttered and the mission became clear. We were reminded that life is not just about "now" but about the sacrifices and hard, right choices made by those who came before us. What's been placed in our hands should be the focus of our lives and what we model and give to the next generation.

Three Outcomes

Verse 7 says that there is a *product*. Why do we pour ourselves into celebrating God's faithfulness and sharing the truth of God's Word with our families and the next generation? Because there is something that we want them to have and become. Look again at the words in verse 7: "so that they should set their hope in God and not forget the works of God, but keep his commandments."

Before we take a look at the three outcomes in this text, I want to underscore that no one can force their children to walk with God. As we said, obedience is not hereditary. Exposure to truth does not necessarily mean that there will be an authentic, vibrant relationship with Christ. Karen and I know couples that are wonderful, godly parents who have lovingly modeled before their children and taught them God's Word. Yet their children have rejected the faith and become prodigals. Salvation and godliness are not the products of some "spiritual behavioral modification" or a relationship we force on our children. We are responsible to do all that we can to create the spiritual environment for our children to respond to Christ, but conversion is work of the Holy Spirit and the expression of *their* faith.

With this in mind, I want to suggest the outcomes mentioned in verse 7 represents our aspiration, what we want to see as a result of what we have intentionally modeled before our children and encouraged them to embrace. We commit ourselves to praying that these things will be their experience and their reality. We are trusting that their marriages and families will pick up the mantle and, in so doing, know the hope and power of God which in turn will produce in them wonderful joy and a sense of mission.

Hope in God

The first outcome is *confidence in God*—"set their hope in God." When our children grow up in a home where there is an active, humble dependence on God, it does something in them and to them. Faith is not theoretical, it is real. They didn't just sit around the table and listen to passages on faith or hear stories about others trusting God to meet their needs. They witnessed their parents bowing before our great God with an open Bible, claiming God's promises and pressing into His faithfulness. And the family was encouraged to join in this journey of faith and dependence.

> Sometimes the best way to help our children is to get out of the way and allow them to trust God.

Notice the direction of the hope (confidence)—it is *in God*. As parents we have to be careful that in our desire to meet the needs of our family we don't send them the message that *we* are the source. We are the channels God uses to provide for their needs, but make no mistake about it, God is the one who sustains all of life and meets all of our needs, including theirs. Reminding our children often that it is God who meets our needs and pausing to express our gratitude to God and to praise Him for His faithfulness will help safeguard us from a sense of entitlement and an unhealthy self-reliance.

The job of all godly parenting is to model trust and dependence on God and to prayerfully raise our children to be "independently dependent" on God. In other words, central to their growth and development is the ability to turn to God and trust Him for themselves. Sometimes the best way to help our children is to get out of the way and allow them to trust God.

Remembering the works of God

This leads us to the second outcome: *a sense of history*, so that we do "not forget the works of God."

Our children are adults now with their own families. They've experienced challenging times. Our two sons have walked through adversity in planting churches and building their ministries. Our daughters, too, have faced and experienced difficulties on their way to fulfilling what God has placed on their hearts. They all have had to work through rough patches in their marriages and the assortment of needs that life and this journey brings to all of us.

At different times each one of our children has said that what has kept them going and encouraged are the memories of God's faithfulness to our family. They remembered when we would gather around the table and pray that God would meet our financial needs. They remembered times when we would open the Word of God and claim His promises to meet our needs. They remembered God's miraculous interventions on our behalf. They remembered the answered prayers. These God-stories have provided them hope and stability as they have been called to trust God during dark, uncertain times.

Our youngest son went through a particularly tough time during the first few years of the church he planted. Finances were tight and there were times he thought they weren't going to make it. He admits that he felt like maybe he should do something else. But as he prayed, God would remind my son of the stories of His faithfulness, and his faith was strengthened and he pressed into the Lord. God proved Himself and met him at his point of need.

Just this morning our oldest daughter called. She has been going through a very challenging time. When I answered the phone, she began to cry. But these were tears of joy. She'd been praying that a particular need would be met, and she was calling me to let me know that once again our faithful God had stepped in and answered prayer.

Some years ago I found out that one of our children had a financial need. When I asked why didn't they let me know, they said they started to call but then remembered the times when we as a family would pray about our needs and how God would come through. Then they said to me, "Dad, I figured it was my turn to trust the Lord to meet this need. And God did!"

An obedient heart

The third outcome is *a will to obey*—"but keep his command-ments." God established a testimony and appointed a law (v. 5) so that we would worship, honor, and obey Him. As we said, God's Word ("law") was not given to us to simply help us to feel better about life and draw motivation from ancient personalities we can identify with. He gave us His Word because He loves us and wants to accomplish His purposes through us. In order to experience what God has for us, we have to cultivate responsive, obedient hearts.

In a sense the treasure we are placing in the hands of each gen-eration is the stories and examples of what God can do through His obedient followers. When we absorb His Word and bask in His faithfulness, we make ourselves available to be used by Him and we become living expressions of His love and power. Likewise, when we choose to discount and dishonor His faithfulness and disobey His Word, we're saying that we know what is best for our lives and we will pick and choose what is right for us. But we're also saying that we do not want God's blessing and favor to be on our lives.

You might be saying, "Boy, that sounds pretty narrow." But think about it. All of life is to be about the glory of God and what He wants to do in and through our lives. He has given us the instructions on how to live and what our mission is in life. And this is the reason why we are charged with passionately and intentionally placing the faithfulness of God and His Word in the hands of each generation.

When we dropped our kids off at college, I gave each of them essentially the same two-word speech: "Obey God."

Again, His proven faithfulness should stir in us an obedient heart. But also we should be aware of the tragic consequences of disobedience. Disobedience at first seems easier and more appealing, to have more of a payoff. But in the long run, disobedience is without exception far more costly than we ever bargained for.

When we dropped our kids off at college, I gave each of them essentially the same two-word speech. I told them that by this point they had heard plenty of speeches and sermons from me. They knew what they had been taught, and they had experienced the faithfulness of God. They knew the Bible, and they knew how to go to it to get the answers they needed. I would lovingly remind them that no one could walk with God for them but them. They own that. Then I would pray with them, kiss them on the cheek, and whisper these two words in their ears, "Obey God."

I am reminded of that scene in Joshua 24 when the Israelites are gathered together there in Shechem to hear the final charge from Joshua. They had seen and experienced the miraculous intervention and favor of God. They knew the tragic consequences of disobedience. Joshua knew that he could not control their

response, but he could make the choice clear. He said in verses
14–15:

> Now therefore fear the LORD and serve him in sincerity and faith-
> fulness. Put away the gods that your fathers served beyond the
> River and in Egypt, and serve the LORD. And if it is evil in your
> eyes to serve the LORD, choose this day whom you will serve,
> whether the gods your fathers served in the region beyond the
> River, or the gods of the Amorites in whose land you dwell. *But as
> for me and my house, we will serve the LORD.* (emphasis added)

We need to keep that choice compellingly clear in our homes
by consistently placing in the hands of our children what matters most.

"God, Please Keep This Going"

When Karen and I visit our adult children, we are moved by their
commitment to place in the hands of their children what we have
given to them. We sit around their tables and listen as they read
the Word of God and bring the needs of their family to the Lord in
prayer. Our hearts are moved by the stories of God's faithfulness.
We find ourselves praying, "God, please keep this going until You
return."

Every day Karen and I pray for our grandchildren. We pray for
their future marriage partners and the children they will have. We
pray that they will know and love the Lord and walk with Him.
We pray that they will celebrate the faithfulness of God and that
their lives and families will be marked by a love for the Word of
God and a desire to obey Him. We also pray for their parents, that

God will give them wisdom and that with all of the demands and distractions of life they will continue to connect with the hearts of their children.

We pray that they will launch their children into the future armed with a passion for God and a commitment that their marriages and families will model the truth about the hope of the gospel and be a source of love and light for their moment in history. "Oh God, do this I pray!"

To think about . . .

We're all aware of the "big" forms of disobedience. But what are some more insidious, subtle ways we tend to disobey God? How could spouses help each other in this?

What are some ways we as a family could weave an awareness of God and His care into our daily lives?

Afterword

Recently, our children and their spouses, along with ten of our grandchildren, spent a week at the beach. This was such a special time. Although we stay connected through technology and visit our children and their families, there is nothing like all of us being together in one place.

As we laughed, played, talked, and spent time praying together, Karen and I were deeply moved by the goodness and blessings of God showered on our family. We found ourselves revisiting the memories, challenges, and some of the difficult times in our marriage. We didn't do things perfectly and we had our share of mistakes, but by His grace we remembered our vows, pressed into the Lord for His wisdom and strength, and watched Him intervene for us—and along the way experienced His love and faithfulness. Now we are watching our children do the same and praying that our grandchildren will be captured by this hope and vision.

Our heart's desire in writing this book is to underscore the reality that marriage affects future generations. The sacred institution of marriage was meant to be an "until-death-do-us-part" commitment. And that's because it is God's heart and intention that marriage serve as an anchor, a portrait of stability and a source of hope in launching future generations. Divorce and dysfunctional marriages, however, have produced a harvest of instability, leaving the next generation wondering if it is possible to find and experience true love, joy, and happiness in marriage. If what we have seen in our homes is so disappointing and unfulfilling, then why would we want to repeat the cycle?

But the cycle doesn't have to be repeated. What we have seen and experienced doesn't have to be our destiny. We don't have to be a prisoner to low expectations and the disappointment of failed and fractured marriages and relationships. No, we can have a marriage and family filled with love, hope, joy, and fulfillment. *God can change the direction of your life and your future.* He did it for Karen, He did it for my mother, and He is doing it for thousands of others. It is not where we came from that ultimately determines the outcome of our lives and choices; it is our response to an all-knowing, all-powerful God that makes the difference. Indeed, our response to Him will determine where we end up.

God sent His Son to pay the penalty for the sin in our lives, to empower us to overcome sin, and to make us new (2 Cor. 5:17). This gospel breaks the chains of our bondage to sin, helplessness, and hopelessness—including the hold that sin has on marriage and family. God, through Christ, has given us a new, responsive heart (Heb. 8:10; 10:15–18). This means that we have the capacity and the power to move beyond the disappointing and destructive influences of our past and embrace with joy and confidence all that God has in store for us, including experiencing His plan and purposes for marriage.

Karen and I know many couples whose backgrounds are not only less than ideal but who also grew up witnessing seemingly everything a marriage and family should *not* be. Yet they have thriving, Christ-centered marriages. Jesus Christ transformed their lives and placed in them the desire to commit themselves to following Him and His plan for their lives and for their marriage.

I think of the woman whose father was married multiple times. She spent most of her childhood years bouncing back and forth between her mom's and dad's houses. Most of the time she felt like a bargaining chip, witnessing their total disdain for each other and having to listen to why the other person destroyed the marriage. Marriage represented pain, and she didn't want to have anything to do with it. And she certainly didn't want to repeat or experience the negative drama she grew up with.

But when she was in graduate school, a friend shared the gospel with her, and she committed her life to Christ. As she began to grow in her faith and spend time reading and studying God's Word, her heart and outlook changed. She met and fell in love with a young man who, too, was a committed follower of Christ. She began to realize that she indeed did not have to become what she saw. It was possible to know love and joy in marriage. They got married, and twenty years later not only do they have a loving, stable marriage, but they lead a Bible study for young married couples.

God is in the business of changing lives and giving us a fresh, new start. And no matter what your background, no matter the mistakes and poor choices you have made, Jesus Christ offers us hope and the power to change.

As we pointed out in the first chapter, the wedding ceremony should be a wonderful, joy-filled event. We are there to support the couple and celebrate their love for each other as they step into the future together. But the wedding ceremony is intended to be a sacred, historic occasion because a *marriage* is taking place. This means that the couple is entering into a covenant, a sacred, solemn, binding agreement. Not only are they pledging to give themselves completely to each other (Gen. 2:24–25) in pursuing and living out their commitment to be one, they are being commissioned, through their marriage, to bear and reflect God's image and model and share the hope of the gospel.

So then, marriage, as we have said throughout the book, is not just about two people enjoying life and making each other happy. Every marriage is a model and a message. Marriage is designed to say something, become something, and initiate something beyond where we are today and touching and shaping a future we will not experience. Marriage is about today and tomorrow. Marriage is intended to be a living, dynamic expression of the person and work of Jesus Christ (Eph. 5:22–33). It is intended to be an inviting model of what the power and love of Christ can do in transforming our lives and serving as a portrait of hope and encouragement. Marriage is the foundation and the cornerstone for the family and future generations.

In short, marriage is mission. Once again, every marriage impacts the future. Marriage is the sacred conduit by which the image of God is passed on from one generation to the next. This implies at least two things. One, we have to be intentional in honoring God in our marriage and in how we raise our children. Second, this can be no casual pursuit. It requires a sense of urgency. It's sobering to realize that how we treated each other, what we believed and taught our children (or what we didn't teach them), and how we lived all this out (or didn't) will either put wind in their sails as they face their future or be a weight holding them back from facing life with hope, confidence, and joy.

We want to encourage you to stay focused on your marriage and family. Don't get distracted. Keep in mind what matters most and what we are placing in the hands of the next generation. Trust the Lord to give you what you need as you face the inevitable trials of life. As a couple, give your marriage and your children the greatest gift you could ever give them: your vibrant, committed walk with the Lord. Keep your heart tender and responsive to God.

Let's keep in mind that God has given us marriage and the family to serve as models to a watching world of what the image, plan, and purposes of God look like, and to influence and commission the next generation to embrace the mission and to do the same. Oh God, do this for our marriages and families, we pray!

—CRAWFORD and KAREN LORITTS

About the Authors

CRAWFORD and KAREN LORITTS met at Cairn University and married in 1971. They have four children—Bryan, Heather, Bryndan, and Holly—and eleven grandchildren. Crawford has authored 10 books and is the senior pastor at Fellowship Bible Church in Roswell, GA. He is the host of two national radio programs: *Living a Legacy* and *Legacy Moments*. Karen is a teacher, mentor, and international speaker as well as a founding member of a foundation that helps those in need work toward a better future. Crawford and Karen are featured speakers at Family Life marriage conferences and are the coauthors of *Building Character in Your Children*.

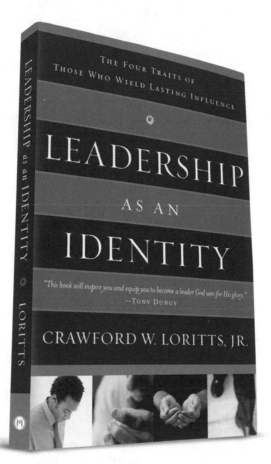